Resources for Teaching

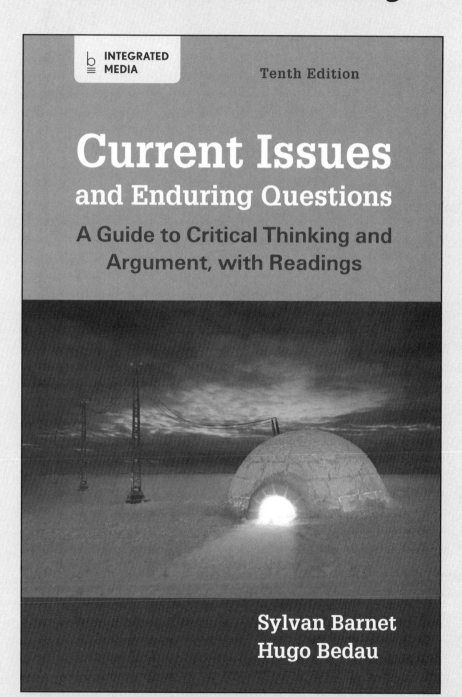

INTEGRATED MEDIA

Tenth Edition

Current Issues
and Enduring Questions
A Guide to Critical Thinking and Argument, with Readings

Sylvan Barnet
Hugo Bedau

Current Issues and Enduring Questions

A Guide to Critical Thinking and Argument, with Readings

Current Issues and Enduring Questions

A Guide to Critical Thinking and Argument, with Readings

Tenth Edition

SYLVAN BARNET
Professor of English, Tufts University

HUGO BEDAU
Professor of Philosophy, Tufts University

Bedford/St. Martin's

Boston • New York

Manufactured in the United States of America.

8   7   6   5   4   3
f   e   d   c   b   a

For information, write: Bedford/St. Martin's, 75 Arlington Street, Boston, MA 02116
(617-399-4000)

ISBN 978-1-4576-6153-2

Preface

These notes, like the book they accompany, are the work of two people—one a teacher of literature and composition, the other a teacher of philosophy. No single set of notes can fully satisfy all instructors or even be of much use to all instructors, but we hope that our alliance enables us to produce material that has something of interest for almost everyone.

THE SCOPE OF THESE NOTES

If the two of us succeed in being of some use, it is partly because we have different approaches and partly because we do not methodically treat every anthologized essay the same way. We treat all of the essays and literary works, but we treat some briefly, some extensively, some chiefly from a rhetorician's point of view, and some chiefly from a philosopher's point of view. We consistently keep in mind, however, the fact that because teachers of composition courses devote many hours to reading students' papers, they have correspondingly fewer hours to devote to working up the background for unfamiliar essays. We therefore provide fairly extensive background on some topics, notably animal rights and immigration, so that an instructor who happens to be relatively unfamiliar with a topic nevertheless can teach with ease the essays we reprint.

Beyond providing background on specialized topics, in these notes we simply touch on various matters we discuss in our classes. We realize that something is artificial here: What you do in class depends heavily on your students and also on the stage in the course at which you are discussing an essay. Further, what you do in class depends even more heavily on your ideas of what teaching is. Still, we hope you will scan these comments and find at least some of them useful; if the comments seem utterly wrongheaded, they may nevertheless be useful in providing material to react against.

THE SYLLABUS

All instructors have their own ideas about how to use the text in a composition course. Which essays are assigned, and in what sequence and at what pace, depends partly on whether you require a short research paper, several short research papers, or a long research paper. Still, our suggestion (for what it is worth) is to teach the first six chapters (Parts One and Two) in sequence.

Part One: In Chapter l we would glance fairly briefly at Jena McGregor's essay and would spend more time on Harlan Coben's "The Undercover Parent." We say we would spend more time on Coben's essay not because it is better written or is more interesting or more important, but simply because Coben's essay is followed by letters of response, and we would ask students to write their own letters, imagining as an audience the readers of Coben's essay. Coben's topic is one that allows students to offer opinions based on experience.

In Chapter 2 we would deal briefly with Susan Jacoby's essay (it is examined at some length in the text) and would spend considerably more time on the three essays that constitute the casebook on free speech. We certainly would discuss, in Chapter 2, the student's essay on the Pledge of Allegiance, and again, we would ask students to evaluate it and to explain why they would give it the grades they do. Such discussion, obviously, will help you to understand what students' ideas are concerning good and bad writing. In Chapter 3, we probably would teach two or three of the eight essays. Notice that Chapter 3 includes an essay on student indebtedness (Webley's) and two essays on Facebook—topics later addressed by a pair of essays on indebtedness (Chapter 14) and a casebook (Chapter 23) on Facebook. You may want to introduce these topics now and return to them later, or you may want to teach these essays later if you teach the debate or the casebook.

To cover Part One (Chapters 1–4) will take about four meetings if, at the beginning of the course, you give only brief writing assignments, or five or six meetings if you require substantial writing to accompany the reading assignments. In our discussions of these chapters in this manual, we offer a few suggestions about essays printed later in the book that go well with the early chapters, but we don't think it is necessary to supplement these first three chapters.

If in teaching Chapter 3—on syllogisms, evidence, and so on—you wish to inform students about the Toulmin model, you will want to supplement Chapter 3 with Chapter 8, which is devoted to that topic. Also relevant to Chapter 3 is Chapter 9, A Logician's View: Deduction, Induction, Fallacies, a fuller and somewhat more difficult discussion of topics set forth in Chapter 3. Our suggestion is this: If you have strong students and you wish to emphasize the role of logic in persuasive writing, assign Chapter 9. Otherwise, skip Chapter 9.

We also would spend part of a class hour discussing the images in Chapter 4, in particular Dorothea Lange's Migrant Mother and the anonymous poster entitled "Our Homes Are in Danger Now!" partly because students enjoy discussing them and partly because later in the term, we may ask our students to analyze images in the casebooks.

Part Two: Although Part One includes a discussion of writing (especially concerning annotating and summarizing), our chief discussion of writing is in Part Two (Chapters 5–7): writing an analysis of an argument, writing an argument, and using sources to write a research paper. Each chapter in Part Two can be covered in a meeting, but you probably will want to give two meetings to Chapter 5, Writing an Analysis of an Argument—one to discuss Nicholas Kristof's editorial and the student's analysis of it, and another to discuss the arguments in at least one of the other essays included in the chapter. In connection with these chapters on writing an argument—especially in connection with Chapter 6, where we talk about the audience as a collaborator—you may also want to assign Chapter 10 in Part Three, A Psychologist's View: Rogerian Argument.

Part Three, Further Views on Argument, contains three chapters already mentioned, A Philosopher's View: The Toulmin Model (8), A Logician's View: Deduction, Induction, Fallacies (9), A Psychologist's View: Rogerian Argument (10), it also contains three additional chapters, A Rhetorician's View (11), A Literary Critic's View (12), and A Debater's View (13). The chapter on literary criticism can stand alone, but it is especially useful as preparation for some of the readings in Part Six, Enduring Questions: Essays, a Story, Poems, and a Play.

Part Four, each chapter of which contains a pair of sharply opposed arguments, lets students examine strong, for the most part unnuanced, statements. If Rogerian argument interests you (it is the subject of Chapter 10), you may want to examine one or more of these debates in Rogerian tems, inviting students to search for common ground, in effect asking them to act as mediators or facilitators.

Part Five offers seven casebooks on current issues (for example, the purposes of a college education, the possible value and the possible danger of hydraulic fracturing, the pros and cons of governmental regulation of junk food). Each issue is represented by several voices, in no case fewer than four arguments, and in one case by as many as nine, including an advertisement with an illustration.

Part Six offers three enduring questions (What Is the Ideal Society?, How Free Is the Will of the Individual within Society?, and What Is Happiness?). These chapters include some literary material: poems by W. H. Auden, T. S. Eliot, Thomas Hardy, Langston Hughes, and Mitsuye Yamada; a short story by Ursula Le Guin; and a one-act play by Susan Glaspell. If you teach some of this literary material, you may also want to assign by way of preparation Chapter 12, A Literary Critic'sView.

Although any essay in the book can be taken by itself, we hope that you will assign most or even all of the essays within at least one thematic chapter (Chapters 19–28), But of course good arguments can be made for being highly selective, and again, much depends on the abilities of the students and on your overall aims.

EXERCISES

All of the essays and literary selections in the text are followed by exercises, but in these notes, we include some additional topics for discussion and writing.

Contents

PART FIVE CURRENT ISSUES: CASEBOOKS 69

27   How Free Is the Will of the Individual within Society?   112

28   What Is Happiness?   120

Part One

CRITICAL THINKING AND READING

1
Critical Thinking (p. 3)

Although the ideas in this introductory chapter are pretty straightforward, many of them will be new to some students, and we have therefore tried to illustrate them with a fairly extended discussion of just one example—the West Virginia law in 1989 that restricts a driver's license to those over eighteen, unless they are still in school, in which case they are eligible for a license at sixteen.

It's extremely instructive to see that sometimes a great deal can be extracted from very little—in this instance, from one statute on a perfectly ordinary matter. We've tried to present in the manageable scope of this humdrum example many of the considerations discussed in greater detail elsewhere in the book. This example gives the student a real taste of what critical thinking, reading, and writing involve, as well as of what lies ahead in the rest of the book.

Bruce Eric Kaplan

He Saves All His Critical Thinking for My Behavior (p. 4)

We reproduce this cartoon because we think it is amusing, and of course what makes it amusing is largely the fact that it sets forth a concept of "critical thinking" that is exactly the opposite of the kind of critical thinking we recommend in the text. The text emphasizes the importance of questioning *one's own* assumptions, but the man in the cartoon clearly does *not* question his assumptions; rather, according to the caption, he questions the behavior (and presumably the assumptions beneath the behavior) of his wife. His stance and his facial expression—especially his down-turned mouth—clearly indicate his self-confidence and his disapproval of the world around him.

The Florida Case (p. 4)

First of all, it may be helpful to remind students that the First Amendment to the U.S. Constitution says, "Congress shall make no law respecting an establishment of religion, or prohibiting the free exercise thereof."

Now for the veil case in Florida. We confess that we don't understand the judge's decision. In our view, it is unreasonable to require a photograph on the license on the grounds that the state has a compelling need for persons to carry an ID. Neither the state nor the federal government requires an ID of all citizens and aliens resident in the United States, and indeed tens of thousands of people in Florida do not carry a photo ID. These people include not only those who do not drive but also those who do legally drive on the basis of a driver's license issued by one of the fourteen states that do not require a photograph on the license.

As our second question (in Topics for Critical Thinking and Writing) implies, we are also uneasy about the logic of saying that although this plantiff is *un*likely to cause harm, she must remove the veil because *other* veiled persons might cause harm.

1

In our draft of the text manuscript, we had a third question along these lines: "Some strict Islamic countries prohibit women from driving. Can it therefore be argued that if Ms. Freeman is a sincere Muslim, she should not seek a driver's license?" We dropped this question because it seemed to us that the rules of certain Islamic countries are not necessarily relevant to the beliefs and actions of a Muslim in this country, but conceivably the question might be raised in class.

According to newspaper reports, American Muslims were divided about the case, and indeed it took the Council on American-Islamic Relations several months before it reached a consensus supporting Freeman, agreement that the state was violating her religious freedom. Among the opinions offered by Muslims were these:

- Islamic law does not oblige women to cover their faces in all circumstances.

- She could have her photo taken by a woman, and if stopped by a male police officer, she could explain the issue and request that he call a female police officer, to whom she would then show the license.

- She could unveil for the picture because she tried her best to follow God's will.

- She could unveil for the picture because Muslims need to support the U.S. national security efforts.

- She is drawing bad publicity for Muslims, and this episode is getting in the way of more important civil liberties where Muslim rights are being attacked.

- She is right to refuse; the court is infringing on religious liberty.

A very different but, in a way, faintly related matter: While we were working on this material, we happened, by sheer chance, to be reading a collection of essays, *The Visual Culture of American Religions* (2001), edited by David Morgan and Sally M. Promey. This book contains an essay by Promey in which she mentions (p. 40) that in 1997, a coalition of Muslim groups wrote a letter to the justices of the U.S. Supreme Court asking them to remove from Adolph Weinman's frieze in the North Courtroom (1931–1932) the face on an image of Muhammad. The image appears with those of other lawgivers, such as Moses, Confucius, and Napoleon. The relevant part of the relief is reproduced on page 41 of Promey's essay.

Islamic art, within a religious context, rarely represents living forms—such representation is thought to be a sacrilegious imitation of the work of Allah—and even more rarely does it represent holy figures. On the rare occasions when Muhammad is shown, his face is veiled, and sometimes his body is represented by a halo of light. One can easily grasp, then, the distress experienced by most Muslims who may see the relatively realistic image in the frieze. Nihad Awad, for instance, director of the Council on American-Islamic Relations, had told the Court that he viewed the image as "sacrilege." At the risk of seeming facetious or blasphemous or both—we are neither; we are in earnest—we might compare the response of a Muslim to the unveiled Muhammad with the response of a devout Christian who might somehow encounter a frontal representation of a nude adult Jesus. The Court replied with a letter from Chief Justice Rehnquist, dated March 11, 1997, saying that the image of Muhammad would not be changed because "it was intended only to recognize him, among many other lawgivers, as an important figure on the history of law . . . [and not] as a form of idol worship." The Court did, however, order a change in the brochure distributed to visitors to the Court. Promey quotes part of the description, but by means of Google we summoned up the whole brochure. (Just type "courtroom friezes north and south walls," and you will get it.) The revised description of Muhammad runs thus:

> Muhammad (c. 570–632) The Prophet of Islam. He is depicted holding the Qur'an. The Qur'an provides the primary source of Islamic Law. Prophet Muhammad's teachings explain and implement Qur'anic principles. The figure above is a well-intentioned attempt by the sculptor, Adolph Weinman, to honor Muhammad and it bears no resemblance to Muhammad. Muslims generally have a strong aversion to sculptured or pictured representations of their Prophet.

Again, the issue of veiled women is different from the issue of representing the Prophet, but conceivably it may come up in class. You may want to ask your students to write letters representing their views of what the Court's letter should have said.

Speaking of courts and religion, for a comment on question 3 in the text concerning a monument of the Ten Commandments in a courtroom, see p. 6 in this manual.

Drivers' Licenses and Dropouts (p. 9)

An update on the issue of preventing dropouts from holding drivers' licenses before they are eighteen: We have been told that several states have found that confiscating the licenses of dropouts does *not* keep youngsters in school and taking away the licenses of failing or disruptive youngsters does not spur them to better work or to better behavior. In fact, some teachers say it is counterproductive because it turns the teacher (in the view of these students) into even more of an enemy than is usual.

Steve Jeffries

Play Ball! (student essay) (p. 12)

We briefly discuss this essay in the text, so we need not spend much time here, though we want to add a few points.

First, although our own view about the issue of homeschoolers participating in public school extracurricular activities differs from Jeffries's view, we think this is a very good essay—thoughtful, clear, effectively written. We do, however, have a mixed response to the title. When we first saw the essay, we liked the title—and we continue to think it has merit—but on reflection, we wonder if "Play Ball!" (a term associated with baseball) goes well with an opening paragraph that is devoted to a football player. Does it set up the expectation that we will hear something about baseball and thus disappoint the reader?

To our brief discussion of the opening paragraph, we would add that in our view, the sentences are shapely and interestingly balanced. Notice, for instance, that the longish penultimate sentence (twenty-eight words) in this paragraph is effectively followed by a short decisive sentence (six words).

The second paragraph is devoted to setting forth the opposing views. We cannot think of any significant objection that it ignores, and, given the imposed limitations of space, we believe it does a good job of stating the objections.

Our chief objection to the essay, perhaps oddly, is that Jeffries pretty much limits his discussion to extracurricular sports. We think he might have strengthened it—been more appealing to academic folks like us—if he talked about letting homeschoolers participate in those kinds of activities, *including academic subjects,* that public schools offer but home-schooling usually cannot. For instance, if his argument had said that, yes, homeschoolers in effect opt out of certain things because their families believe they can cover those things better than the public school can. But there are of course certain kinds of things that homeschooling cannot do as well. For instance, chemistry probably cannot be taught effectively at home, and, similarly, Chinese probably cannot be learned at home unless a parent reads and speaks Chinese or is willing to hire a tutor. That is, we think the essay might have been stronger—might have been more appealing to *us*—if the argument covered academic work as well as extracurricular activities. The overall angle would be that it is in the interest of *society* to let homeschoolers participate in public school activities when homeschooling cannot offer the appropriate facilities. We probably would be more likely to go along with the idea of letting homeschoolers play on the baseball team if we thought they might also take the public school chemistry or Chinese course.

Harlan Coben

The Undercover Parent (p. 21)

In the text itself, we offer our own paragraph-by-paragraph discussion of the rhetoric of Coben's essay, and rhetoric—the art of using language persuasively—is what we think should be the primary subject of the discussion in a composition course rather than the issue that Coben addresses. But yes, we also recognize that the rhetoric is *about* something that it is used in the service of arguing a particular cause. The cause Coben advocates is probably unpopular with adults, as his first paragraph indicates. We have never taught this essay: It will be interesting to hear how students respond. Our guess is that many students will think that Coben is making a good point.

You or your students may find that our analysis in the text is defective in one way or another. If so, the class can have a good time pointing out its inadequacies and can thereby learn that not everything they read in print is true. But if you think our analysis is a satisfactory interpretation of the ways in which Coben makes his point, you may want to turn directly to the topics that we offer, or to issues that students raise in class. (Our own favorite pedagogical practice when we teach an op-ed piece is is to ask students to write a response.)

Jena McGregor

Military Women in Combat: Why Making It Official Matters (p. 28)

We address, in sequence, the topics that we set forth in the book.

1. McGregor's tone: We think readers will agree that McGregor appears to be unpretentious, reasonable, fair-minded, a person of goodwill, not a one-sided bullying advocate. Indeed, at least at the beginning, one almost thinks one is reading a news report, a narrative ("Last week, female soldiers began formally moving into jobs in previously all-male battalions") rather than an argument. But of course the piece *is* an argument, and this is indicated at the very outset, in the subtitle: "Why Making It Official Matters."

   The tone throughout is thoughtful and courteous (e.g., "Another way to break down the ceiling would be," "But . . . it's easy to see," "Both changes may be difficult"), and we believe that even readers who ultimately are unconvinced will nevertheless agree that McGregor is, as we have just said, reasonable and fair-minded.

2. The term *brass ceiling* by means of a rhyme, of course, plays on the term *glass ceiling*, the transparent barrier that lets women (in the business world) see the higher echelons but keeps women from reaching them. The barrier in the military is here called *brass* because the insignia of commissioned officers (the admiral's gold stripes, the general's stars) are colloquially called *brass*, as in "the top brass will never approve of this."

3. McGregor does *not* mention one argument that is sometimes offered against putting women into direct combat: A captured female soldier might be raped. You may want to invite your students to discuss the strengths and weaknesses of this argument. When we raised the issue, the general response was that the argument had no weight at all: (a) Captured men, too, can be raped, and (b) captured men and women can be tortured and killed. So given the circumstances, the issue of possible rape is hardly decisive. Still, even if your students raise these responses, we think it is worth discussing whether McGregor should have introduced the argument and then briefly rebutted it.

4. The argument concerning body strength is almost always present in discussions of the issue of women in combat. In comparing such matters as upper-body strength

or bone density of men and of women, one of course is speaking in generalities, not about particular individuals. But the gist is (as we say in our fourth topic in the text), some people argue that in some circumstances, women—again, we are speaking in general—are less competent than men are. Usually, in discussions about women in combat, upper-body strength is cited, and the standard examples concern pulling a wounded comrade out of a tank or off a battlefield. The idea is females are OK as, say, tank mechanics behind the lines, but not as members of a tank crew. We assume everyone would agree about the difference in upper-body strength, but we have also encountered the statement that when males enter competition, their testosterone level rises, increasing their hemoglobin and hence (this is getting complicated) their blood's capacity to carry oxygen, thus heightening the brain's sense of confidence and appetite for risk (the so-called *winner effect*). In short, heightened testosterone supposedly heightens courage. We have no idea if any of this business about testosterone = courage = a better fighter on the battlefield is true.

In any case, putting aside the issue of whether women should be allowed on the frontlines, we see the force of McGregor's argument that battlefield experience should not be a requirement for top command. Surely the requirement is a vestige of antiquated macho thoughts about what war is.

5. Presumably, the change in policy—women are now allowed to be in combat—makes women eligible for the top posts; so presumably, (a) the possibility of a military career is more attractive to the best and brightest women and (b) as McGregor points out, there may indeed be more diversity of thought at the top (the assumption here is that diversity of thought is a good thing because it may lead to wiser decisions).

6. As for whether—if there is a national draft—women should be drafted, well, discuss. (Please notice that we devote a casebook, Chapter 25, to the issue of whether young people should be required to perform public service.)

Exercise 3 *(p. 32)*

As we mention earlier in this manual in connection with the case of the Muslim woman vs. Florida, a frieze in the Supreme Court depicts Muhammad, along with Moses and other lawgivers, so there is some sort of precedent for introducing religion into the courthouse.

In the wee hours of the morning on July 31, 2001, Chief Justice Roy Moore of the Alabama Supreme Court had a 5,280-pound granite monument that was engraved with the Ten Commandments placed in the lobby of the Alabama Supreme Court. Civil liberties groups sued, arguing that the monument violated the First Amendment, which prohibits the government from supporting religion. Judge Moore insisted that the Ten Commandments are the basis of the secular law of our country. In November 2002, Federal District Court Judge Myron H. Thompson ordered Moore to remove the monument. Thompson noted that the excerpts from Exodus 20:1–17 (and also with slight differences in Deuteronomy 5:6–21) are a Protestant version of the commandments (the translation Moore used is the King James Version). Jewish, Roman Catholic, Lutheran, and Eastern Orthodox scriptures use slightly different versions of the Ten Commandments; so the version in the courthouse seems to endorse one particular faith, though (as we say in the text) the judge and his supporters say that the monument is a symbol of the roots of American law, not an endorsement of one religion.

A very few words about the differences may be useful. The Roman Catholic and Lutheran churches combine (take as one commandment) the passage forbidding the worship of other gods and the passage forbidding the making of images, and they treat as two commandments the prohibition in Exodus 20:17 against coveting a neighbor's wife (the ninth commandment) and house (the tenth). Most Protestants and Eastern Orthodox

Christians take the first commandment to be "You shall have no other gods before me" and the second commandment to be the injunction against the making of images. Modern Jewish usage counts verse 2 as the first commandment and verses 3–6 as the second.

When the federal judge ruled that the monument must be removed, there was considerable public protest. Rev. Patrick Mahoney of the Christian Defense Coalition and Rev. Rob Schenck, president of the National Clergy Council, led supporters to Montgomery, where they kneeled en masse in front of the monument. A round-the-clock operation was begun, with people unfurling bedrolls on the courthouse steps.

Moore is no stranger to controversy. When he was a circuit court judge in Gadsden, he hung a wooden plaque with the commandments in his courtroom. It generated controversy—enough controversy to encourage him to run as "the Ten Commandments judge" in 2000 in his successful campaign for chief justice. When the associate justices unanimously overruled the chief justice, he was temporarily removed from presiding over the court, pending a trial by the Alabama Court of the Judiciary.

The last time that the U.S. Supreme Court ruled on a case concerning government display of the Ten Commandments was in 1980, in *Stone v. Graham*. Stone was one of a group of parents who challenged a Kentucky law that required all public schools to post the Ten Commandments in every classroom. The money for the printed commandments was provided by private sources, and each copy said, at the bottom, "Secular application of the Ten Commandments is clearly seen in its adoption as the fundamental legal code of Western civilization and the Common Law of the United States." The Court, however, rejected (five to four) this argument, holding that just because Kentucky said that its law had a secular purpose did not make it so. And it rejected as irrelevant the fact that private funds were used.

Justice Rehnquist, in a dissenting opinion, wrote:

> The Supreme Court should defer to the State in determining the secular purpose of postings. The State Legislature and State Courts both believe that the postings have a secular purpose, and the Court should respect this; especially given that the secular purpose, the "Ten Commandments have had a significant impact on the development of the legal codes of the Western world," is acknowledged to be true.

Back to Judge Moore: On August 21, 2003, the eight associated justices of the Alabama Supreme Court overruled Moore, their chief justice, and unanimously ordered that the monument be removed from the lobby. Starting the next day, a fine of $5,000 a day was to be imposed if the monument remained in public view. Moore had been told by the federal judge that he could display the monument in his private chambers, if he wished.

Here are two interesting complications concerning the display of the Ten Commandments in or on a courthouse. (1) As we mention in our discussion of the Florida veil case, the image of Muhammad appears on a frieze in the U.S. Supreme Court. The image of Moses also appears there, holding the Ten Commandments as part of a display of lawgivers, including Hammurabi and Confucius. The courts have ruled that this sort of display of the Ten Commandments within a court is acceptable because it is part of a larger historical display. (2) On August 13, 2003, a federal appeals court in Pennsylvania refused to reconsider a ruling that allowed a 1920 plaque with the Ten Commandments to remain on the façade of a courthouse in suburban Philadelphia. The three-judge panel of the Third U.S. Circuit Court of Appeals had ruled in June that the plaque did *not* constitute an official endorsement of religion because the county commissioners who wanted to keep it were moved by an interest in historic preservation, not religion.

It is probably true—at least Gallup Polls suggest this—that most Americans consider the Ten Commandments as valid rules for a good secular life, but few can give a moderately accurate rendition of even half of the commandments. And in any case, the argument that the commandments are a symbol of the roots of American law, not an endorsement of one religion, seems odd when one remembers that the very first commandment concerns monotheism, the second prohibits the making of "graven images" (by the way, how many Americans adhere to this commandment?), the third prohibits taking the Lord's name in vain, and the fourth concerns observing the sabbath. True, the remaining commandments (concerning respect for parents, killing, adultery, stealing, perjury, and covetousness) are more evidently secular, but even these are ultimately rooted in a particular theology.

We will let Judge Moore have the next-to-last word. According to a report in the *Boston Globe,* August 21, 2003, on CBS's *The Early Show* he said:

> This case is not about politics or religion. It's about the acknowledgement of God. . . . We must acknowledge God because our Constitution says our Judicial system is established upon God.

The last word: A special ethics panel (appointed by various legal organizations, the Alabama governor, and the lieutenant governor) on November 13, 2003, unanimously voted to remove Chief Justice Roy Moore from the Alabama Supreme Court. (The panel's vote was binding only if unanimous.) A topic for argument: Should an *un*elected panel have the power to remove an elected judge?

EXERCISE 4 *(p. 32)*

In addition to arguments concerning aesthetics and cost, the chief argument seems to be that a barrier is not effective: People who want to commit suicide will find other sites where they can kill themselves. That is, according to persons who hold this view, the bridge does not cause suicide, it does not tempt people who otherwise would not commit suicide. Further, it has been argued that barriers might actually increase the number of people who jump to their deaths because barriers would drive such people to other locations—let's say a cliff or a tall building— where there is no possibility that they would be talked out of their acts. Apparently, a considerable number—but we don't have the statistics—of potential bridge-jumpers are persuaded not to jump.

2
Critical Reading: Getting Started (p. 34)

The major points made in this chapter—that one should read carefully and that making a summary helps one to grasp an argument—are obvious, and perhaps that's why students often ignore them. Our experience suggests that students often fail to grasp the main points of an argument not because it is especially difficult but merely because they do not read it carefully. But if they do read it carefully (aided by writing a summary), they are likely to find ideas arising—differences with the author. Therefore, the process of writing a summary of someone else's ideas can be a way of generating ideas of one's own. Drawing on the assumptions in Chapter 1, it may be useful to ask students to underline any explicit assumptions that the writer makes (these will probably appear in the summary) and then to think about, and to jot down, any assumptions present but *not* stated.

Susan Jacoby

A First Amendment Junkie (p. 47)

With Susan Jacoby's essay, we hope to show that even where the language is informal, the topic is familiar, and the argument is fairly easy, a second or third reading may reveal things not perceived in a quick scanning.

At this stage in the course, we are less intent on exploring the pros and cons of the issue than on teaching how to read, how to summarize, and how to become aware of explicit and implicit assumptions. "How to read" includes developing awareness of persona and tone, and it is worth discussing the title (even though it is the editors', because the original title was simply "Hers," the unvarying title of a weekly column in the *New York Times*), and worth discussing the ways in which Jacoby establishes a persona.

Although in the text we do not discuss the role of a persona until Chapter 5, preliminary discussion in class can help to pave the way for the students' later encounter with the topic. Because a writer's choice of a persona depends partly on the audience, it is appropriate to discuss this essay *as an argument for readers of a specific newspaper.* It's not a bad idea to ask students to read a couple of issues of the *Times.* Students who have been taught to write in a somewhat stiff, impersonal manner may be surprised to learn from Jacoby (and other columnists in the paper) that they can use "I" and that they can even use colloquial diction ("junkie") in some contexts.

Our second question in the text, on Jacoby's next-to-last paragraph, is prompted by our thought that although the essay is always clear, she makes some leaps. The women who favor censorship in paragraph 1 are, on the whole, women who see pornography as one kind of violence against women. Paragraph 5 gets into kiddie porn—a related issue, but not the same issue. Jacoby probably introduces it to dissociate herself from the extreme position of some opponents of censorship. (It is usually a good idea to distance oneself from extremists who share one's views.) But the issue of young people surfaces again in paragraphs 13 and 14. There is, of course, a connection between Jacoby's arguments that parents should protect the young and her argument that adult-oriented pornography, however objectionable, should not be censored. The connection is that it is the job of adults to fulfill their responsibilities, and not to "shift responsibility from individuals to institutions" (para. 13).

Question 3, on the final paragraph, aims at getting students to see that a final paragraph need not begin "Thus we see" and need not summarize all the points argued earlier.

Question 5, about what is or is not permitted under the "absolute interpretation of the First Amendment," is meant to provoke some thought about whether anyone does or should want the free-speech clause to include protection of offensive and possibly harmful acts—when the acts are wholly verbal (as seems tolerated by Justice Black's remark quoted in Jacoby's para. 2). Falsely shouting "Fire!" in a crowded theater may be no more than a speech act, but it was Justice Holmes's famous example of speech *not* protected by the First Amendment because in a context of utterance such as his example provides, these words would cause "a clear and present danger" of *harm* (and not merely annoyance, offense, or other hostile feelings) to the innocent.

For a discussion of constitutional law on the First Amendment, see Archibald Cox, *Freedom of Expression* (1981). An older book, still of great value, is Thomas I. Emerson's *The System of Freedom of Expression* (1970). A somewhat more recent book on the subject is by Anthony Lewis, *Make No Law* (1991).

Note: We discuss in the text, on page 50, Jacoby's essay from the point of view of the Toulmin method.

Zachary Shemtob and David Lat

Executions Should Be Televised (p. 53)

In stating the objections to their view that (to quote the title of the essay) "Executions Should Be Televised," the authors insist (para. 13) that they do not assume (with Sister Helen Prejean and other foes of capital punishment) that visibility would engender revulsion against the practice and thus would stimulate support for opposition to capital punishment. The authors, claiming to be open-minded, say that they advocate making executions public simply because (to quote their final paragraph), "A democracy demands a citizenry as informed as possible about the costs and benefits of society's ultimate punishment."

To our ears, this statement does not quite ring true. We can't understand how seeing a televised image of an execution—whether the criminal dies with a smile or a grimace on his or her face, whether his or her body is contorted or apparently relaxed—gives us much information "about the costs and benefits of society's ultimate punishment." We somehow cannot escape thinking that Shemtob and Lat oppose capital punishment and think (like Prejean and others whom they name) that if the public could see it put into practice, the public would be so repelled that it would oppose the punishment. That is, we think there is an underlying irony here: The authors argue, with a straight face, that executions should be televised so that the public can be better informed, but the reader—well, the writer of this page in this instructor's handbook—believes that their proposal is so monstrous that its real purpose is to engender opposition to capital punishment. (Yes, we use the word *proposal* because we we wish to evoke thoughts of Swift's "A Modest *Proposal*," which similarly offers a monstrous argument with a straight face.)

Maybe. Or maybe some folks would take pleasure in witnessing a painful death. Here's something to think about. Thomas Macaulay (1800–1859) famously said, "The Puritans hated bear-baiting, not because it gave pain to the bear, but because it gave pleasure to the spectators." Macaulay was being witty, taking a poke at what he assumed were pleasure-hating Puritans. But can't a good case be made that indeed we ought not to take pleasure in certain kinds of things (in Macaulay's comment, setting dogs upon a chained bear)? If this is true, and if we think that some viewers will relish the spectacle offered by executions, well, then, shouldn't such spectacles be banned? Discuss. (We return to this point in our discussion [p. 26 in this manual] of Nora Ephron's essay of photographs of a woman falling to her death.)

Gwen Wilde (student essay)

Why the Pledge of Allegiance Should Be Revised (p. 56)

We begin by saying that we would give this essay an A. We think it is clear, thoughtful, and courteous—on a subject that has engendered plenty of intemperate writing. Admittedly, the title is not especially engaging, but it has the merit of clearly announcing both the topic and the thesis, and for those reasons we think it is not bad.

The first paragraph is informative, probably telling most readers something they did not know (that the original version of the Pledge did not include the words "under God"). The next paragraph advances the necessary information—that the phrase was added in 1954—and the paragraph ends with an explicit statement of the thesis:

> In my view, the addition of the words "under God" is inappropriate, and they are needlessly divisive—an odd revision for a Nation that is said to be "indivisible."

If we had written the sentence, we probably would have used *because* instead of *and* ("because they are needlessly divisive" rather than "and they are needlessly divisive"), but that's a small point. What we like about the student's sentence is the wordplay involved with *divisive* and *indivisible.*

Wilde goes on to question the meaning of President Eisenhower's words—we ourselves find them a bit fuzzy—and she then points out (para. 5) that "in the Pledge patriotism is connected with religious belief." She goes on to give a reason for suggesting that even though a large percentage of Americans believe in God, the words "under God" do not belong in the Pledge ("several million Americans do *not* believe in God").

We find especially interesting her brief discussion (para. 9) of the use of the motto "In God We Trust" on American coinage. Given Wilde's position on the words "under God" in the Pledge, we would have guessed that she would also object to the motto on coins. Presumably, she introduces this issue—effectively, we believe—to show that she is *not* a fanatic who objects to every tiny hint of religion in American public life.

The quotation from Associate Justice David Souter lets the reader know that Wilde has done some homework, and her comment on the quotation shows that she is thinking carefully about the quotation. In her final paragraph, she reiterates her thesis, but she manages not to be merely repetitive. For instance, in this paragraph she introduces the information that "the Founding Fathers . . . never mentioned God in the Constitution." But perhaps what especially animates this final paragraph, in which there is little new information, is the note of urgency, for instance, when Wilde says, "Yes, they [students] can remain silent when others recite these two words, but, again, why should they have to remain silent?"

A week or two after we drafted the material that you have just read, we came across some comments by Ronald Dworkin on this topic (as well as on intelligent design and on gay marriage) in the *New York Review of Books* (September 21, 2006). Dworkin finds the Pledge "coercive," but he adds, "That coercive impact, however, is in fact not very strong and so though the official Pledge is a violation of liberty it is not a practically serious one." Dworkin goes on (as in fact the student did) to introduce a comparison with the pious words on our coinage, but unlike the student, Dworkin thinks the words in the Pledge are as innocuous as the words on money. Dworkin says:

> Just as an atheist can fish in his pocket for a coin that bears a message of trust in God or stand at the opening ceremony of prayer in congressional or court sessions without any sense of self-betrayal, so he can mouth the words of the Pledge, or skip the words he finds objectionable, without loss of integrity. (p. 28)

Our own view, for what it is worth, is that Wilde is right in thinking that a child reciting the Pledge is *not at all* like (to quote Dworkin) "an atheist fish[ing] in his pocket for a coin that bears a message of trust in God." The atheist—unless he or she is dedicated to removing every vestige of religion—probably hardly thinks of the words when fishing for a coin, but a child reciting the Pledge must be thinking of the words, whether he or she recites them or remains silent.

Discuss.

A Note on Hate Speech

The argument about whether hate speech (for example, racial epithets) should be permitted on the campus is not likely to go away, nor is it likely to be answered definitively. Here are the chief arguments that we have encountered.

Arguments in favor of restricting speech on the campus:

1. Speech demeaning a person's color, creed, sex, sexual orientation, or other personal attributes creates a hostile learning environment—a workplace in which work cannot be done—and thus such speech infringes on the rights of others. Sometimes this argument is supported by being compared with sexual harassment: The courts have upheld regulations against sexual harassment in the workplace. Thus, if women have a right to work in a nonthreatening environment, then students have a right to study in an atmosphere free of racial (or other) harassment. But how exact is the comparison?

2. Limitation of such speech is allowable under the "fighting-words" doctrine. A face-to-face insult using four-letter words or other epithets addressed to an individual or a small group is not intended to discover truth or initiate dialogue; rather, it is an attempt to injure and inflame. Such language is not protected by the First Amendment, according to the Supreme Court in *Chaplinsky v. New Hampshire* (1942). (In this case, a man shouted into the face of a police officer that he was a "Goddamned racketeer and a damned fascist.")

3. A college or university fosters unlimited inquiry, *not* unlimited speech. Hate speech does not lead to advances in knowledge.

4. Outlawing hate speech would not mean that there would be limitations on discussions even of heinous ideas in situations that allow for rebuttal or for persons to choose not to attend.

Arguments against restricting speech on campus:

1. Restrictions against remarks about race, creed, and so forth, violate the rights of free speech under the First Amendment. Such remarks do not come under the fighting-words doctrine because it is not clear that they will produce violence, especially if they are comments about groups rather than specific individuals.

2. By tolerating (rather than suppressing) such speech, we are in a better position to diagnose the real problems that give rise to racist speech and can try to face them directly, not indirectly through regulation and prohibition.

3. We all need to develop a thicker skin to merely verbal utterances that offend. If we don't, then either we will foolishly attempt to protect *everyone* from whatever speech offends them, or we will yield the platform and rostrum to whoever is nastiest among us. Either way threatens disaster; the best remedy for bad speech is still better speech, not silence.

4. Exactly which words are to be prohibited? When three students at the University of Wisconsin complained that they had been called *rednecks,* the administration told them that *redneck* is "not a demeaning term." Or consider the word *Negro,* once considered a polite term, used by African Americans both privately and publicly, but now regarded by many as demeaning. Another example: *Queer* used to be, and for many people still is, a demeaning term for a homosexual, but in the last few years, many homosexuals have used the term, as in the group called Queer Nation.

11

The Supreme Court decided (June 1992) that an ordinance against hate speech enacted by the city of St. Paul was unconstitutional. The ordinance banned any action "which one knows . . . arouses anger, alarm, or resentment in others on the basis of race, color, creed, religion or gender." The case did not concern speech on the campus, but it did concern expression of racial hate—the burning of a cross on the lawn of a black family that had recently moved into a white neighborhood. In *R.A.V. v. St. Paul,* Justice Scalia, writing for the majority of five (Kennedy, Rehnquist, Scalia, Souter, Thomas) held that government may not opt for "silencing speech on the basis of its content."

The majority opinion, holding that the St. Paul ordinance was impermissibly narrow, acknowledged that hate speech directed at race or religion was hurtful but did not concede that there was any difference in kind between a racial epithet and, for instance, an insult directed at union membership or political affiliation. The court made the point that burning a cross on someone's lawn is "reprehensible," but it insisted that "St. Paul has sufficient means [such as trespassing laws] to prevent such behavior without adding the First Amendment to the fire."

The other four justices agreed that the St. Paul ordinance was unconstitutional, but they would have struck it down on the less-sweeping ground that it was written in too broad a manner. The justices who did not sign the majority opinion (Blackmun, O'Connor, Stevens, White) were troubled by the refusal of the majority to see that certain kinds of hate speech are especially evil. Justice White, for instance, said that the city's

> selective regulation reflects the city's judgment that harms based on race, color, creed, religion, or gender are more pressing public concerns than the harms caused by other fighting words. . . . In light of our nation's long and painful experience with discrimination, this determination is plainly reasonable.

Justice Stevens, in a footnote, glancing at the Los Angeles riots earlier in the year, wrote:

> One need look no further than the recent social unrest in the nation's cities to see that race-based threats may cause more harm to society and to individuals than other threats. . . . Until the nation matures beyond that condition, laws such as St. Paul's ordinance will remain reasonable and justifiable.

In short, the justices who refrained from joining the majority valued free speech not as something good in itself but as something instrumental. That is, they valued speech on the ground, that it serves a constructive purpose by helping to create a better informed electorate and therefore a better country. In this view, speech that is harmful need not be protected.

According to a report in the *New York Times* (June 24, 1992), a spokesperson for the American Council on Education said that the consequences of the decision for colleges and universities were unclear. Private institutions faced fewer constitutional restraints, the report said, than did public institutions, but it was thought that those educational institutions with codes would probably modify them. For instance, after a federal court in 1989 declared unconstitutional the code of the University of Michigan in Ann Arbor, the university adopted a provisional code prohibiting

> physical acts or threats or verbal slurs, invectives or epithets referring to an individual's race, ethnicity, religion, sex, sexual orientation, creed, national origin, ancestry, age, or handicap made with the purpose of injuring the person to whom the words or actions are directed and that are not made as part of a discussion or exchange of an idea, ideology, or philosophy.

You might want to ask your students to evaluate the Michigan provisional code.

A CASEBOOK FOR CRITICAL READING:
SHOULD SOME KINDS OF SPEECH BE CENSORED? (p. 60)

Preliminary Note: Free Speech in the Age of YouTube

Our heading, "Free Speech in the Age of YouTube," is the title of an article in the *New York Times* by Somini Sengupta (September 23, 2012). We summarize Sengupta's piece here.

Companies are usually accountable only to shareholders, but Internet companies—because they deal in speech—must make decisions about what kind of expression is allowed. In September 2012, a video mocking Mohammad circulated on YouTube (owned by Google) and provoked a storm of protest in the Islamic world. An attack on the American Embassy in Libya resulted in the death of the ambassador and three other Americans.

The question: Should Google allow access to the video in Libya (or in other Muslim countries)? Google in fact then restricted the piece in Libya and in six other countries where it is unlawful to show disrespect for the Prophet.

Two additional points:

- Apple and Google ordinarily obey the laws of countries in which they do business.
- International law does *not* protect speech designed to cause violence.

A CASEBOOK FOR CRITICAL READING:
SHOULD SOME KINDS OF SPEECH BE CENSORED? (p. 60)

Susan Brownmiller

Let's Put Pornography Back in the Closet (p. 61)

First, a point made by Wendy Kaminer in an essay in *Take Back the Night*, edited by Laura Lederer (the book in which Susan Brownmiller's essay also appears): In recent years, feminists such as Brownmiller have been arguing that pornography is not merely dirty (obscene) but is, by virtue of images of violence against women, a threat to society. The distinction, Kaminer explains, is important. "Obscenity" is not constitutionally protected, but it is very narrowly defined. According to the Supreme Court ruling in *Miller v. California* (1973), obscene material is material "that the average person, applying community standards . . . would find . . . as a whole, appeals to the prurient interest" and "taken as a whole, lacks serious artistic, political, or scientific value." It is extremely difficult to prove in court that a work is obscene. Moreover, although almost any piece of hard-core pornography probably fits this description, enforcement of obscenity laws is difficult because the government may not prohibit publication of any material before the courts decide it is obscene. Each book or magazine must individually be judged obscene before it may be enjoined. Kaminer points out that a store with one thousand books cannot be closed because of fifty or even five hundred obscenity convictions. The stock that has not been judged obscene can be sold.

The newer view of pornography, developed especially by Catharine MacKinnon and Andrea Dworkin, sees it not merely as obscenity but as material that depicts the subjugation of women. Pornography is said to represent violence against women, thereby impeding their chances of achieving equal opportunity. It should be mentioned, by the way, that although some feminists oppose pornography on the grounds that it is humiliating to women, other

13

feminists argue that (1) modern feminism is itself linked to sexual liberation, and (2) feminists who fear pornography unwittingly reinforce the notion that women are sexually passive.

Brownmiller, claiming that the battle for free speech has on the whole been won, asserts that pornography is not chiefly a matter of free speech; but she, like MacKinnon and Dworkin, politicizes the issue and thereby tends to legitimize pornography. That is, by seeing it as political speech, these writers bring it into a constitutionally protected area. Of course if they can demonstrate that pornography is a threat to society—a "clear and present danger"—then they will have put it in an area not constitutionally protected, but it is very difficult to prove that something is a "clear and present danger" (cf. question 3).

A February 1986 ruling of the Supreme Court is relevant. The Court ruled *un*constitutional an Indianapolis ordinance that forbade pornography on the ground that it is a form of discrimination against women. The ordinance, drafted with the help of MacKinnon and Dworkin, defined pornography as "the graphic sexually explicit subordination of women, whether in pictures or in words," if it showed them enjoying "pain or humiliation" or if they were in "positions of servility or submission or display." Brownmiller is especially concerned about images of these sorts. Although the Supreme Court did not explain why it declared the ordinance unconstitutional, perhaps we can guess the rationale by considering the explanation of Judge Frank Easterbrook, for the court of appeals, when he ruled against the city ordinance. Easterbrook said that the Indianapolis law "discriminates on the grounds of the content of speech" by establishing "an 'approved' view of women." "This is thought control," he said, for this law attempted to silence explicit speech that did not conform to a particular view of women. He also pointed out that the law could be applied to Homer's epics and to Joyce's *Ulysses*.

Now to look, briefly, a little more closely at Brownmiller's essay. She begins by calling free speech "one of the great foundations on which our democracy rests," thus putting herself on the side of virtue, a good strategy when arguing. Brownmiller then goes on to indicate that she would not burn *Ulysses, Lady Chatterley's Lover,* and the *Tropic* books. Again she is on the side of virtue, or at least of classic liberal thought. In short, Brownmiller devotes her first seven paragraphs to showing that she is for democracy and the arts. In paragraph 8 she says she is "not opposed to sex and desire," again establishing her credentials as a liberal. In paragraph 9 she briefly explains why feminists *do* object to pornography (it degrades women), and the remainder of the essay (less than half of the total) amplifies the point. In paragraph 14 she raises an important point that we mentioned earlier in this commentary—not all speech is protected. But as we suggested, although the Constitution does not protect a person who falsely shouts "Fire!" in a crowded theater (a "clear and present danger"), there is some question about whether pornography represents such a danger. Still, by mentioning false advertising and the cry of "Fire," paragraph 14 effectively suggests that pornography is not necessarily protected.

Charles R. Lawrence III

On Racist Speech (p. 64)

In recent year, so-called hate speech on campus has provoked anger and dismay among students, faculty, staff, and the public at large. Any attempt to control such speech by official regulation seems likely to be on a collision course with the First Amendment. Or so most academic administrators concluded, after *Doe v. University of Michigan* (1989). In that case, regulations restricting free speech on the Michigan campus, arising out of a desire to resist "a rising tide of racial intolerance and harassment on campus," were permanently enjoined by Judge Avern Cohn. Judge Cohn had no difficulty permitting regulations as to time, place, and manner of speech. His concern was about the way the university's regulations governed *content*. He held that any regulations against the content of "speech" on no stronger ground than that it was "offensive"—even "gravely so [to] large numbers of people"—was unconstitutionally vague and overbroad.

Charles R. Lawrence is himself African American (see his para. 15) (by the way, he's the brother of Sara Lawrence Lightfoot, author of the widely acclaimed *Balm in Gilead: Journey of a Healer* [1988]), and he presents a measured defense of narrowly drawn regulations against hate speech. No enemy of the First Amendment (see paras. 1 and 14–19), he nonetheless doubts whether its defenders really will act on the proposition, touted by the American Civil Liberties Union in its perennial defense of the First Amendment, that the best remedy for bad speech is more and better speech (para. 17).

Lawrence's position (question 2) is clear from the opening sentence of paragraph 8: If regulations of conduct on campus are needed to protect minority students from harassment and personal vilification, then "equal educational opportunity" is the "compelling justification" for them. We would agree; a few students have no right to make campus life intolerable for others by language, gesture, or symbol that interferes with their rightful access to all the campus has to offer.

But we would also urge that before any such regulations are adopted, one needs to reflect carefully on several basic facts. Everyone finds some words or pictures offensive, but what offends one does not always offend others. Not everything that is offensive is seriously harmful (or counts as harassment). Finally, not everything offensive can be prevented. We all need to develop a thick skin to the merely offensive, lest we find ourselves provoked into violent response or timidly cowering before verbal bullies. We all also need to cultivate a civil environment, free of insulting, degrading, and offensive behavior, verbal or otherwise, especially on a college campus.

Part of what makes the whole hate speech issue so controversial and difficult are the uncertainties that surround the key words "assaultive speech," "verbal vilification," and the like (question 4). Lawrence does not attempt to define these terms explicitly, nor does he provide illustrative and convincing examples of verbal conduct that is "assaultive" or "vilifying." (Students could be usefully asked to give such examples—genuine or hypothetical—and then see whether they can give sensible definitions of these terms.) Nor does Lawrence draft a model set of regulations for hate speech that would prevent (or make liable to punishment for) the harm such speech causes and still pass constitutional muster.

We suspect that Lawrence would deny that straight white males are as vulnerable to insulting posters and the like as are certain other classes of students (blacks, women, gays). The reason is that political power and social status have traditionally been the preserve of white males so that as a class they are relatively immune to the power of offensive language to degrade and intimidate. Of course, Lawrence might still argue (as we would) that straight white males ought not to have to endure insults because of their race or sexual orientation and that regulations protecting women or blacks or homosexuals from vilification ought to be extended equally to all classes of students.

Derek Bok

Protecting Freedom of Expression on the Campus (p. 69)

Like Charles R. Lawrence III (see the previous essay in the chapter), Derek Bok is trained as a lawyer, avows his personal allegiance to the First Amendment, and speaks from a position of concern about racially provocative speech and symbols on a private university campus. (This last point is important because the courts seem to agree that *private* colleges and universities are not bound by the First Amendment, as are public institutions. Notice that in paragraph 9, Bok rightly refuses to use this reason for favoring regulations of free speech on the Harvard campus.) But where Lawrence speaks in measured tones on behalf of the victims of "hate speech," Bok seems to speak for the vast majority of bystanders, those who are neither victims nor offenders where hate speech is concerned.

Bok offers three very different reasons for opposing attempts to curtail hate speech. First, unlike Lawrence, he is doubtful whether the class of harmful verbal and graphic symbols can be suitably defined so that they can be regulated without infringing on full freedom of expression (para. 10). Second, even if such regulations could be drafted and enforced, they would not change racist attitudes or bring greater mutual respect and decency to campus life (para. 11). Finally, irrepressible adolescents will gleefully "test the limits" of these regulations, thereby aggravating the nuisance and trying the patience of deans and disciplinary committees (para. 12). From our own experience, we are strongly inclined to agree with Bok on all these points, even if they do not constitute the last word on the subject.

What constructive measures against hate speech does Bok recommend? First, prospective victims ought to learn to "ignore" nasty and hateful speech; second, the rest of the campus community ought to counsel and persuade would-be vilifiers to mend their ways, lest they do grave harm to some of their fellow students (para. 13). Sensible advice, indeed—but perhaps too easily issued by one who himself is neither black, female, gay, or (it would appear) in any other way a member of a group specially vulnerable to verbal assault. Indeed, we can understand how some will judge Bok's counsels to be unimaginative and deeply disappointing.

Notice, too, that although Bok cites several grounds for restricting speech (para. 7), they do not include the ground Lawrence mentioned in the previous essay—namely, ensuring equal educational opportunity to minority students.

Pedagogical Note: One case study that students have enjoyed exploring in relation to Bok's essay is the topic of flag burning.

If some students do see the American flag as sacred, as something that is desecrated when it is burned by angry protestors, do they also see the Confederate flag as sacred, as something that deserves special protection? You might remind them (or inform them) that the Confederate flag (or a variation) has flown over the capitol buildings of some southern states and has evoked strong protests. In the early months of 2000, for instance, the National Association for the Advancement of Colored People (NAACP) organized a boycott of South Carolina because the Confederate battle flag was displayed over the state's capitol. For some citizens, the flag celebrated the "southern heritage"—for instance, the gallantry of Confederate soldiers. For others, most obviously the NAACP, the flag offensively celebrated slavery. Incidentally, a compromise was reached that satisfied almost no one: The flag was removed from the capitol building and was flown elsewhere on the capitol grounds.

3
Critical Reading: Getting Deeper into Arguments (p. 74)

This chapter may seem to hold our major discussion of arguing, for in it we talk about definitions, assumptions, induction, deduction, and evidence (and we do think it is essential reading for students), but we think that the upcoming three chapters —Writing an Analysis of an Argument, Developing an Argument of Your Own, and Using Sources—are equally important. Moreover, for especially strong students, Part Three will be valuable. It includes a summary of the Toulmin method for analyzing arguments and then offers further discussion of deduction and induction from a philosophic point of view. It also includes a survey of fallacies (Chapter 9), Carl R. Rogers's "Communication: Its Blocking and Its Facilitation" (Chapter 10), and Max Shulman's entertaining and informative "Love Is a Fallacy" (Chapter 9).

Nothing is particularly difficult in the chapter; most students should have no trouble with it.

Note: In our discussion of *analogy* we give Judith Thomson's example in which (during the course of an argument on abortion) she invites the reader to imagine that he or she wakes up and finds that a violinist whose body has not been functioning adequately has been hooked up to the reader's body. Thomson's essay originally appeared in *Philosophy and Public Affairs* 1.1 (Fall 1971): 47–66, and is reprinted in her book *Rights, Restitution, and Risk* (1986).

George F. Will

Being Green at Ben and Jerry's (p. 107)

We discuss this essay at length in the text, so there is no need for much additional comment here. We do want to say, however, that you may find it useful to discuss not only Will's essay but also our comments on it: We will not be surprised if students (and some instructors) markedly disagree with our observations. We think the piece is engaging, largely because it is so entertaining. In our view, what makes it at least moderately persuasive is not so much the statistics (though these do have some power) but the wit that pervades the essay and (we confess sheepishly) the hint of scatology in those sentences about the mound of manure and the bag of flatulence. As we say in the text, Will's final paragraph says nothing about oil or the Arctic National Wildlife Refuge, and thus it might seem ("'seem?' nay, 'is!'") irrelevant, but it is entertaining and, alas, a bit of humor may outweigh a good deal of earnest logic. Having said this—and we continue to believe that much of Will's effectiveness here is in his wit—we want to say again that he does have other arrows in his quiver, such as statistics.

Apparently the problem of bovine burps and flatulence continues to be serious and will get worse because the production of beef and milk is expected to double in the next thirty years. It turns out that the most damaging aspect of the milk industry (from an environmental point of view) is not the burning of fossil fuels for transportation or packaging, but the emissions of cows—200–400 pounds of methane a year per cow. (Methane is second only to carbon dioxide as a heat-trapping emission associated with global warming.) The *New York Times* ran an article ("Greening the Herds," June 5, 2009, p. A12) about some dairy farmers who are making an effort to reduce the methane output of cows. These farmers have adjusted the diet of the herds, diminishing the amount of corn and soy and increasing the amount of alfalfa and flaxseed. The results are said to be very encouraging, but the feed now costs more, so there is some uncertainty about whether this practice will be widely imitated.

Stanley Fish

When "Identity Politics" Is Rational (p. 114)

Consider the definition of "identity politics" that Fish offers in his first paragraph. If we follow the guidance we offer in *Current Issues* on the best way to write a definition, we get something slightly at variance with what he offers. Thus, we would say that one engages in identity politics if and only if one votes for or against someone or something because of his or her skin color, ethnicity, religion, gender, sexual orientation, or any other marker that leads one to affirm or deny what someone says independently of that person's reasons, ideas, or politics. A bit of a mouthful, to be sure, but it captures the essential idea of a good definition, namely, that it be neither too broad nor too narrow.

Fish identifies two different forms of identity politics in paragraph 9: The tribal version and the interest version. He argues that the tribal version has little to recommend it (there are, he admits, rare exceptions to this generalization). As for the interest version, he sees no alternative to it. If you can't rely on your considered judgments, on what can you rely? Fish devotes paragraph 10 to a good account of his answer to this implicit rhetorical question.

Gloria Jiménez (student essay)

Against the Odds, and against the Common Good (p. 118)

We think this is a first-rate essay—thoughtful and effectively written. The title has a nice parallel: The first sentence is informative and sensible, and the second sentence, though long, is shapely and easily readable. We think this long sentence is readable partly because it begins with a strong signal at the start (the transitional word *Still*), because it contains a parallel ("bringing a bit of excitement . . . bringing a vast amount of money"), and because it ends with an independent clause ("the states should not be in the business of urging people to gamble"). The second paragraph amplifies the point, again with a clear transition (*and*, plus a word—*urge*—picked up from the previous sentence). The organization of the entire essay also, in our view, contributes to its clarity: The opening states the thesis clearly; arguments in favor of lotteries are then presented lucidly (in fact, they are numbered); and we are told which are the less important arguments (discussed first and relatively briefly) and which are more important (discussed last and relatively fully).

Jiménez's idea of putting some emphasis on the slogans strikes us as especially interesting. Anyone can talk, rather generally, about the pros and cons of the issue, but she has shrewdly presented some highly engaging sentences ("There Is No Such Thing as a Losing Ticket") and then discusses their implications. She has also done a little research so that she can offer effective details rather than mere opinions.

In our first question in the text, we do raise what we think is a significant point. Jiménez neglects to discuss a common argument: If our state doesn't run a lottery, our citizens will just gamble in the lottery of some other state, so we will lose revenue and gain nothing. We don't know what Jiménez's response would be, and we are not sure even of our own, but we are inclined to think along these lines: (1) Although some people—those who live near the border of the state—will gamble in the lottery of another state, many will not; (2) if gambling is wrong, especially because the majority of people who gamble are the ones who can least afford it, the state should not sponsor it in any case, even if adjoining states do sponsor it.

Our second question in the text asks if readers find the essay a bit "too preachy." (This was the response of one of our students when we showed her the essay.) We don't see it that way. Admittedly, the essay is highly schematic and takes the high moral ground, but we think the tone is engaging ("an almost sure-fire way of getting nothing for something," "dreams of an easy buck," "It's against the odds," "an activity that is close to pickpocketing"). Our chief uneasiness—and we want to say again that we think this is a first-rate essay—is with the somewhat solemn introduction of the first person: "I now get to the point in my argument." "I say that this argument is delicate," "Let me end a bit indirectly." On the other hand, we do tell students that there is nothing wrong with using the first person and that obvious evasions ("It has been argued in this paper") usually are not the way to go. Perhaps Jiménez might have reduced the use of the first person slightly—for instance, by saying "This argument is delicate" rather than "I say that this argument is delicate"—but we want to reiterate that we think the essay is excellent.

Anna Lisa Raya (student essay)

It's Hard Enough Being Me (p. 121)

As we weigh in our headnote in the text, Anna Lisa Raya published this essay while she was an undergraduate. Your students may very well find that they can do just as well.

If you have looked at the questions that we pose in the text, you have probably guessed that we think Raya is a bit unclear about *why* she "had to define [herself] according to the broad term 'Latina'" (para. 2). The closest she comes, we think, to offering an explanation is when she says that in "El Sereno, I felt like I was part of a majority, whereas at the College I am a minority" (para. 2).

But even this sentence, we think, doesn't say *why* she "had" to define herself. Pressure from the majority? From the minority? Again, she says (para. 8), "To be fully Latina in college . . . I *must* know Spanish." But (again) *who* demands that she be "fully Latina"? As we read the essay, we are inclined to guess that the demand comes from Latinos and Latinas who emphasize their heritage and want Raya to celebrate it, but we don't think she is explicit on the point. She ends by asserting—briefly, in Spanish and in English—that she will be herself. We think this ending is rhetorically effective since it uses both languages.

There is, however, a further difficulty. Exactly what does it mean to be true to oneself? Of course, we can say that we don't steal (we are not that sort of person) or that we don't cheat (again, we are not that sort of person). But isn't "the self" really constructed out of relationships to others? We are loving (or neglectful) parents or children, we are serious (or frivolous) students, we are serious (or casual) about advancing in a career, and so on. We have many selves (parent, child, student, worker), and it is not always easy to know *which* self we must be true to.

Ronald Takaki

The Harmful Myth of Asian Superiority (p. 123)

In his first paragraph, Ronald Takaki introduces the term *model minority,* a term our fifth question asks students to consider. Takaki couples this term with being financially *successful,* and it's our impression that when Asian Americans are said to be a *model minority,* the term does usually imply financial success, conjuring up images of prosperous merchants, engineers, lawyers, and so on. But it's our impression, too, that the term also implies three other things: academic success (strong undergraduate work and graduate or professional work), family stability, and a low crime rate. Takaki is scarcely concerned with these matters, though in paragraph 7 he mentions "gangs" of Asian Americans (an indirect glance at crime), and in paragraphs 8–10 he touches on Asian American laborers—though it turns out, in paragraph 12, that some Korean greengrocers are highly educated.

Chiefly, Takaki is concerned with disproving the myth of financial success, and he wants to do this for two reasons: The myth is harmful to Asian Americans (because the rest of America mistakenly thinks this minority is doing very well), and it is harmful to African Americans (because the rest of America uses the Asian Americans as a stick to beat the African Americans). To demonstrate that the financial success of the Asian Americans is a myth, Takaki introduces statistics—and indeed it is partly because of his statistics and because of his comments on the possible deceptiveness of some figures that we include Takaki's essay in this chapter. As early as his fourth paragraph, he points out that statistics may be misleading. He doesn't cite specific figures, but he says (convincingly, we think) that it's not enough to point to "figures on the high earnings of Asian Americans relative to Caucasians." Why not? Because, he says, Asian Americans tend to be concentrated in places with a high cost of living (Hawaii, California, New York). This is a telling point. Again, even without giving specific figures, he sets the reader thinking, giving the reader cause to be skeptical about the figures.

The bulk of the essay (paras. 4–14) is devoted to the finances of Asian Americans, but surely Takaki's purpose in demythologizing Asian Americans is twofold: to say something that will help Asian Americans and to say something that will help African Americans. Although African Americans are mentioned in only paragraphs 3 and 15, their appearance is significant, especially because one of the two appearances is in the final paragraph.

This essay makes use of statistics and also calls attention to the misuse of statistics. You may want to invite students to examine Takaki's statistics. We wonder, for instance, exactly how significant it is that "twenty-five percent of the people in New York City's Chinatown lived below the poverty level in 1980" (para. 8). For the figure to be meaningful, one would probably have to know what percentage of the rest of America lived below the poverty level in 1980. And in any case, why cite a figure from 1980 in an essay written in 1990? That's a long time ago; surely there must be a more recent figure.

You may want to invite the class to bring in some statistics on this or another issue, perhaps gathered from an article in *Time* or *Newsweek* or from a textbook, and to discuss their possible limitations.

James Q. Wilson

Just Take Away Their Guns (p. 125)

Our question 1 goes to the heart of this essay: What sentence in James Wilson's essay best expresses his thesis? We suggest the answer is in this sentence in paragraph 4, when Wilson writes: "The most effective way to reduce illegal gun-carrying is to encourage the police to take guns away from people who carry them without a permit." Why do we focus on this sentence? First, it echoes the title of the essay ("Just Take Away Their Guns"). As we suggest elsewhere in the text, a good title will often signal the writer's main thesis. Second, the quoted sentence implies that the *goal* of gun control is to get guns out of the hands of those most likely to use them illegally, and that the *best means to this end* is authorizing the police to stop and frisk. Any careful reader of Wilson's essay will see that it is this second point and its ramifications that get most of Wilson's attention in the rest of the article.

Our second question is intended to get the student to look carefully at the research Wilson cites and to evaluate just what that research implies. One cannot infer that displaying or firing guns in self-defense actually prevented victimization in all, most, or even many of the million cases where guns were used for this purpose. Nor are we told in how many of these million cases the gun user was under a misapprehension (no robbery or other crime was in the offing) or in how many other cases children or others in the household caused accidental deaths or injuries by firearms. So on balance, we do not know anything from this research about the extent to which safety in the home was increased (or decreased) by the availability and use of firearms by ordinary citizens to prevent crimes. The only legitimate use of the statistics Wilson reports here is the very limited use he himself makes of them in the final sentence of his paragraph.

How might a defender of gun control respond to Wilson's barb quoted in our question 3? In his twelfth paragraph, Wilson thinks it is "politically absurd" for a citizen in crime-infested America to seek laws that "forbid or severely restrict the sale of guns." This is the preface to his remark we quote in the question.

Before proceeding with a reply, as the question asks, we draw the reader's attention to the extreme and perhaps misleading generalization in his remark quoted above. Are the restrictions and prohibitions to which he refers here confined only to handguns? Or does he think all restrictions on firearms of whatever sort are "politically absurd"? We do not think it is "politically absurd" for the government to forbid outright all sales of automatic weapons, dumdum bullets, antitank weapons, and the like except to authorized purchasers. Perhaps Wilson would agree. If so, he might have easily made that clear.

More to the point, we think the gun-control advocate might reply to Wilson's challenge along these lines:

First, no government can hope to shield its citizens against all criminal harms, even if by deterrence and incapacitation, not to mention moral education, government does keep crime from overwhelming us. (Ask the class: How many of you were the victims of crime earlier today? Earlier this week? This month? How many of you were *not* victims only because you used a weapon to frighten off a would-be assailant?) So it is unfair to describe our "government" as "having failed to protect" our persons and property. Its successes vastly outnumber its failures.

Second, society has to weigh *all* the consequences of our current virtually uncontrolled gun ownership practices against the alternative of varying degrees of restriction and prohibition. It is not enough just to look at the ways in which guns in the hands of the citizenry have deterred crime. Those successes have to be measured against the many costs that Wilson nowhere mentions (notably, suicides and other killings and accidents that would not have occurred except for the availability at all hours of loaded handguns).

In our question 5, we ask the reader to confront the racial impact of Wilson's proposal, which he candidly mentions. We agree with his prediction: Widespread use of stop-and-frisk practices aimed at removing guns from those without permits to possess them will in practice do exactly what he says. Is this a fatal objection to his proposal? Yes, if you think that young black males have enough problems already without the added burden of heightened attention from the police, or that stop-and-frisk practices will lead mainly to more shoot-outs with police on the mean streets of urban America. No, if you think that black neighborhoods are far more likely to be victimized by black offenders than are white neighborhoods, that the best way to protect the bulk of the black population is to get illegal guns out of the hands of would-be black offenders, and that the best way to do this is to encourage adoption of Wilson's stop-and-frisk proposal.

Kayla Webley

Is Forgiving Student Loan Debt a Good Idea? (p. 129)

Our first question in the book asks why, in her second paragraph, Webley makes the point that reading some of the stories retold on the Student Debt site is a heartrending experience. The answer, of course—at least from the point of view of someone writing an argument—is that (to get directly to the point) this author will soon reject the views expressed by the authors of those stories; so at the outset, she wants to express her sympathy, to establish an engaging *ethos* lest she later seem coldhearted. And indeed, at the end of her essay, she again expresses sympathy with Robert Applebaum's idea, though she characterizes it as "wildly unfeasible."

In short, she begins and ends by indicating that her heart is in the right place—but the body of the essay severely criticizes Applebaum's idea. First, she quotes Justin Wolfers's devastating critique (we print it on p. 469). Then she goes on to assert that, in fact, most indebted students *can* repay the loans (paras. 6–7), and in paragraph 8 she talks about alternatives for those who cannot repay the loans. In 9 she raises the issue of fairness: Why should taxpayers foot the bill for college graduates?

In short, she sees no merit in Applebaum's idea—except (and here we get to Webley's final paragraph) that it *is* an idea, and ideas are what is wanted. Thus, although she shreds Applebaum in the body of the essay, she expresses sympathy for debtors at the beginning, and at the end she gives credit to Applebaum for at least offering an idea, even if it is "wildly unfeasible."

The essay ends in a time-tested way by putting the ball in the reader's court: "[W]hat's your solution?" We have often heard our colleagues grumpily say that they do not want their students to use formulas, but in fact real writers—Webley writes for *Time* magazine— often *do* use formulas, time-tested patterns and devices. The important point is that within the formulaic structure, they write carefully, thoughtfully, engagingly.

Later in the book, in Chapter 14, we offer two additional essays on student indebtedness.

Alfred Edmond Jr.

Why Asking for a Job Applicant's Facebook Password Is Fair Game (p. 132)

We were astounded to learn that some employers ask job candidates for their passwords to Facebook, and that this request is legal. But, well, lots of things astound us today. (Reminder: It is *not* legal for a potential employer to inquire about age, race or ethnicity, sex [gender], marital status, pregnancy, religion, or disability.)

Given the fact that (in our view) Edmond is taking an outrageous position, we think he does a pretty good job of defending it. First of all, in his second paragraph he indicates that in other circumstances he would take a different position. Then, with a clear transition at the beginning of his fourth paragraph ("That said, my response"), he begins a defense of his earlier position, and we think he gives a good example, in the fifth paragraph, when he cites "the child care industry." The trouble, from our point of view, is that we cannot think of any other example that is equally forceful. Working in a facility with mentally impaired persons might come close.

The problem, as we see it, is that some (many?) people think they are performing a helpful social service when they reveal highly personal information. Thus, they may think they are helping to break down harmful stereotypes, helping to reduce prejudices, when they reveal to certain persons that, for instance, they are gay or deeply depressed or addicted to certain medicines. In our view, Edmond gives sound advice when he says, "Don't think business vs. personal. Think public vs. private. And if something is truly private, do not share it on social media out of a misplaced faith in the expectation of privacy."

These words of Edmond make sense to us, but we continue to doubt that sense can be made out of his title, beyond perhaps the child care industry.

Addendum: Should Colleges Monitor the Posts and Tweets of Athletes?

The issue is different, of course, but a discussion of Edmond's essay can easily get into related issues of what is and what is not acceptable in posts and tweets. Here we want to summarize a discussion that we came across in *Time*, October 22, 2012, pages 56–57.

North Carolina (UNC) defensive tackle Marvin Austin in 2011 posted something about partying that led the National Collegiate Athletic Association (NCAA) to investigate, and it found that he had received cash gifts. Other athletes on the team also had broken rules, and the NCAA ultimately banned UNC's football team from the 2012 postseason and reduced its allotment of football scholarships for the next three years.

Because some colleges receive a great deal of money from their football program, they of course worry that athletes may inflict damage on the program. Therefore some of these colleges prohibit the athletes from using Twitter. Some colleges permit the use of Twitter but require the athletes (in the words of Utah State University) to "grant full remission for the university and other third-party monitors to gain access to the 'friends only,' 'private,' and similarly designated areas." Such a policy even requires a student athlete to sign a waiver: "To the extent that any federal, state, or local law prohibits the Athletic Department from accessing my social networking accounts, I hereby waive any and all such rights and protections." As *Time* puts it, the university thus requires the student to license the university to ignore the law. On the other hand, some states have offered protection to the students. *Time* reports that California has a law forbidding colleges to "require or request" that a student or prospective student "divulge any personal social media information."

Sherry Turkle

The Flight from Conversation (p. 136)

Turkle's essay is one of many essays we have encountered that express alarm at the alleged harmful effects of social media. There are, of course, counterviews, and we want to begin this brief discussion by mentioning Adam Gopnik's entertaining survey of books on the topic, "How the Internet Gets Inside Us," *New Yorker,* February 14, 2011. Gopnik divides the commentaries into three groups:

> Call them the Never-Betters, the Better-Nevers, and the Ever-Wasers. The Never-Betters believe that we're on the brink of a new utopia, where information will be free and democratic, news will be made from the bottom up, love will reign, and cookies will bake themselves. The Better-Nevers think that we would have been better off if the whole thing had never happened, that the world that is coming to an end is superior to the one that is taking its place, and that, at a minimum, books and magazines create private space for minds in ways that twenty-second bursts of information don't. The Ever-Wasers insist that at any moment in modernity something like this is going on, and that a new way of organizing data and connecting users is always thrilling to some and chilling to others—that something like this is going on is exactly what makes it a modern moment.

Gopnik amusingly illustrates his categories thus:

> When the electric toaster was invented, there were, no doubt, books that said that the toaster would open up horizons for breakfast undreamed of in the days of burning bread over an open flame; books that told you that the toaster would bring an end to the days of creative breakfast, since our children, growing up with uniformly sliced bread, made to fit a single opening, would never know what a loaf of their own was like; and books that told you that sometimes the toaster would make breakfast better and sometimes it would make breakfast worse, and that the cost for finding this out would be the price of the book you'd just bought.

Probably most of us sometimes feel one way, sometimes another way, and sometimes a third way—in Gopknik's terms, Never-Better, Better-Never, and Ever-Waser—which is to say that we think there is something important here, and yet . . . . Take Turkle's eighth paragraph, in which she comments on today's young people in a library, together but each in his or her own bubble. Yes, thinks the Ever-Waser, just like when people in olden decades sat in a library reading books, together but each in his or her own bubble.

One other point: When we first read Turkle's essay, we were briefly puzzled by her reference in paragraph 13 to "the word," and we had to reread a few sentences. She is in fact talking about the word *conversation,* ultimately derived from the Latin verb *convertere,* "to turn around." You may want to ask students to offer conjectures about other words with *vers* in them, for instance, *averse, adversary, diverse, obverse, reverse.*

Note: Chapter 23 offers a casebook (five essays) on Facebook.

4
Visual Rhetoric: Images as Arguments (p. 141)

Dorothea Lange

Migrant Mother (photographs) (p. 167)

We think most students will agree that the more tightly framed image is more moving. The other is interesting, but the lamp in the lower left, the lean-to, the landscape at the right, and the faces of the two children—especially the appealing face of the child resting her chin on the mother's shoulder—provide distractions. In the famous image, which is more symmetrical than the other and almost surely puts us in mind of traditional paintings of the Madonna and child, the two faceless children have turned to the mother for comfort. Further, the mother's hand touches her chin, somewhat suggesting the pose of Rodin's *The Thinker;* but whereas Rodin's muscular man is an image of strength—mental as well as physical—Lange's migrant mother is an image of powerlessness. We can admire her courage, and we know that her children love her because they turn to her for comfort, but we also know that however hard she thinks, she is not going to solve her problem.

A few further points about the image: In 1958, one Florence Thompson (1903–1983), a woman of Cherokee heritage, revealed that she was the subject of the photograph. In 1936, when the photograph was taken, Thompson was the mother of eight childen, two of whom were illegitimate. (She later had three children by a man to whom she was not married.) Question: What might the effect of the photo be if it showed eight children rather than three? Our own view—purely a conjecture, of course, since Lange did not take such a photograph—is that an image showing an impoverished woman with eight children might provoke some thoughts that she was irresponsible. In any case, we find it hard to imagine that a photograph showing Thompson with eight children could have the dignity and the power that the famous image does have.

Among the useful books on Lange are Linda Gordon's *Dorothea Lange: A Life Beyond Limits* (2009) and Anne Whiston Spirn's *Daring to Look: Dorothea Lange's Photographs and Reports from the Field* (2009).

Anonymous

Our Homes Are in Danger Now! (poster) (p. 168)

We think it is interesting that although Hitler is shown, a specific Japanese person (Emperor Hirohito or General and later Prime Minister Tojo) is not shown. Apparently during World War II, no single Japanese face was sufficiently familiar to American viewers to stand for Japanese aggression. Perhaps behind this failure to identify an individual Japanese is the common Western stereotype that "they all look alike."

Why does Hitler have a gun and the Japanese a knife? There is no need to comment on the gun, but probably the knife suggests the racist idea that Asians are more primitive than Caucasians.

The globe that Hitler and the Japanese are grabbing shows the United States, and the text ("OUR HOMES ARE IN DANGER NOW!") is given visual form by little houses on the map. Speaking of little houses, why is the image of the American response—a bomber and a tank, encircled by the words "*OUR JOB* KEEP 'EM FIRING"—so small? Presumably to emphasize our vulnerability. We Americans are the little kids on the block, menaced by hulking bullies.

James Montgomery Flagg

I Want YOU (poster) (p. 169)

We are concerned here less with the medium than with the message. Our concern with the medium is with body language initiated on Flagg's poster. The assertive pointing scarcely needs explanation, but most students will be less aware of the implication of the full-face view, versus, say, a three-quarter view, or a profile. Facial expression is more conspicuous in a front view than in a profile. A profile tends to be expressionless, immutable (that is why it is commonly used on coins and medals), but a front view can more obviously catch the emotion of a moment. Moreover, a front view confronts the spectator, looks into the spectator's space, and suggests an all-seeing and inescapable presence. Flagg's Uncle Sam unreservedly reveals his emotions, dominates us, stares us down. Although the written message ("I want YOU for U.S. Army") is, when you think about it, directed only to potential recruits, Uncle Sam's assertive finger and his penetrating eyes are directed to every viewer; the effect is to make *all* passersby feel guilty, so that they will make additional efforts on behalf of their country.

Two notes: (1) The origin of Uncle Sam is obscure, but he seems to have come into being during the War of 1812. It is said that the name derives from "Uncle" Sam Wilson, an inspector of army supplies. The initials "U.S." (to indicate government property) were stamped on army barrels and crates, but they apparently were taken to stand for "Uncle Sam." The iconography was fixed by the latter part of the nineteenth century; Uncle Sam was tall and lean with white hair and chin whiskers, tall hat with stars and stripes, swallowtail coat, vest, and striped pants. He can be kindly in a gruff way, but for the most part, despite the clownish costume, he is stern and energetic. (2) Flagg eliminated the usual stripes from the hat, and by eliminating the lower half of the body, with its striped pants, he made the figure less extravagant. He modeled the face on his own but took the composition from a British poster by Alfred Leete, which showed the head of Lord Kitchener, the Recruiting General, and a foreshortened hand emerging from a cuff, above the legend "Your Country Needs YOU." Leete's poster is reproduced in John Barnicoat's *A Concise History of Posters* (1969, p. 226), and in Harold F. Henderson's *The Poster* (1968, p. 75). For German and Italian versions of similarly gesturing figures, see Max Gallo's *The Poster in History* (1974, pp. 166–67). See also Robert Phillipe's *Political Graphics* (1982), not only for the illustrations but also for the valuable text. For anonymous parodies of Flagg's poster, produced to oppose the Vietnam War, as well as for a large, color reproduction of Flagg's poster itself, see *Arms and the Artist* (1977), selected by Denis Thomas: No. 94 shows a bandaged Uncle Sam, not pointing vigorously, but weakly extending a hand as if in need of support, with the legend, in Flagg's lettering, "I Want OUT"; no. 96 reproduces Flagg's format, but with Uncle Sam as a skeleton. We have heard of (but not seen) a more affectionate parody, suitable for hanging in a child's room: Uncle Sam, pointing the usual accusatory finger, stares out above the legend, "I Want YOU to Clean Up Your Room."

A comment toward a suggestion for writing: There is yet another aspect to Flagg's message. How do we know the approximate date? That is, what in the *style* lets us know that this poster is from World War I? After all, the hairstyle and the costume of the figure are not a giveaway, as they would be in most old posters and advertisements, and as they are in Leete's picture of Kitchener. It might be interesting to ask a class what approximate date they would give to Flagg's poster, and why. (The poster was created in 1917. It was used again in World War II, but that is irrelevant.) Perhaps the resulting discussion (or essays) will help students understand something of what instructors mean by "style." Our own feeling is that the lettering, indebted to hand-painted signs of the late nineteenth century, clearly belongs to the early part of the twentieth century, and the realistic drawing is characteristic of posters for World War I rather than for World War II. The posters of World War II tended to show, in a very simple way, the influence of cubism and of abstract art; figures, if they were not photographs or close copies of photographs, tended to be flat and even geometric. A face might be a mere plane with no shading, or it might have a strongly demarked shadow, giving it at most only two planes. Often the designs give the effect of a collage or montage, thus further moving away from the tradition of illusionistic drawing.

Nora Ephron

The Boston Photographs (p. 170)

Many people get agitated when images that they take to be pornographic are published in magazines or are hung on museum walls. Your students know this, but they may not know that until quite recently, many people thought that images of violence should not be shown. Respectable newspapers did not show the blood-spattered corpses of gangland killings. That sort of image was left to the tabloids. The chief exceptions were photographs of persons killed in war, but even these were acceptable only if the dead seemed intact and asleep. Severed limbs, decapitated bodies, and agonized faces were not tolerated. But exactly why were they not tolerated?

"All the news that's fit to print" was and still is the slogan of the *New York Times*. And just as some news stories were judged unprintable—let's say stories about prostitution and abortion—so were some images. Probably the idea behind this informal code was that such stories and images pander to a taste that ought not to be nourished. We are reminded of Thomas Babington Macaulay's comment on bearbaiting: "The Puritan hated bear-baiting not because it gave pain to the bear, but because it gave pleasure to the specta- tors." An astute remark, not merely a wisecrack at the expense of Puritans. Why, indeed, do we in the United States prohibit cockfighting in all but two states? Surely not merely because a few birds suffer for relatively brief periods—a tiny number, when compared with the enormous numbers of birds that suffer for months until they have grown large enough to be slaughtered for food. Presumably forty-eight states prohibit cockfighting because their citizens think—rightly—that spectators ought not to take pleasure in the sight of birds maiming each other. The idea is as old as Plato: Our base appetites ought not to be nourished.

To get back to certain kinds of pictures of violence, the idea behind censoring them was that these images appeal to impulses that ought to be suppressed, not nourished. It is pretty hard for anyone today to favor censorship, but when you look at the pictures in James Allen et al., *Without Sanctuary: Lynching Photography in America* (2000), and you learn that some of these horrifying images of burned and castrated bodies were printed as picture postcards and inscribed with playful comments (e.g., "This is the barbecue we had last night"), well, one understands what Plato and the Puritans were getting at.

In our text, the most horrifying image is not reproduced in Ephron's essay but is Huynh Cong (Nick) Ut's photograph on page 146, "The Terror of War" (1972). This picture, which was widely printed in newspapers, is said to have played an enormous role in turn- ing American public opinion against the war in Vietnam. (For details, see Denise Chong's *The Girl in the Picture: The Story of Kim Phuc, the Photograph, and the Vietnam War* [2000].) Conceivably, some people take pleasure in the horror it depicts, but surely its publication was justified by its message: "What is going on over there is unbelievably horrifying." On June 8, 1972, American-backed South Vietnamese pilots trying to kill Viet Cong troops dropped napalm canisters near a pagoda where villagers had taken refuge. The girl in the center of the picture had torn off her clothing in an effort to free herself from the sear- ing napalm jelly. A viewer looks with horror at the picture, but—and we say this with much unease—part of our interest in the photograph probably is aesthetic. In its terrify- ing way, it is a beautiful photograph, admirably composed, the sort of composition that

Henri Cartier-Bresson called "the decisive moment," the moment when the flux of the world suddenly takes shape and seems to say something. The four figures nearest to the camera run forward, but they take us back relentlessly. The boy at the extreme left shows his agony in his wide-open mouth and his slightly contorted posture; the naked girl in the center, vulnerable in her nudity, is by virtue of her outstretched arms in a posture that reminds a viewer of the crucified Jesus; the small boy toward the right (like the smaller boy who is the second figure from the left) is apparently too young to understand the horror, but the girl who holds his hand reveals her terror in her face. And behind them, apparently walking rather than running, apparently a relentless and unemotional force (we can see no expression on their faces) pushing these victims forward, are four soldiers (one is almost totally hidden by the girl at the right). And still further back, behind the soldiers, is a flat backdrop of the smoking village.

Is this photo merely an image of a most regrettable incident—like, say, a fire in Boston that kills a woman who falls from an unstable fire escape? Or does it have meaning? And, if so, what is its meaning? Ephron doesn't talk about this image, but she does make a relevant point in her next-to-last photograph, when she talks about car wrecks and says that newspapers will print images of wrecked cars but not of dead bodies: "But the significance of fatal automobile accidents is not that a great deal of steel is twisted but that people die. Why not show it?" And in her final paragraph she introduces an aesthetic element when she says, of the Boston photographs, "They deserve to be printed because they are great pictures, breathtaking pictures of something that happened. That they disturb readers is exactly as it should be: that's why photojournalism is often more powerful than written journalism."

In short, although doubtless there are some people who enjoy the violence depicted in some images, images of the sort that Ephron is talking about (photos by Stanley Forman) and images like Ut's rivet our attention because—one can hardly dare to say it—the horror is transformed by the artistry. This is *not* to say that the horror is diminished. Far from it; the horror is made memorable, enduring, and perhaps even eternal.

Part Two

CRITICAL WRITING

5
Writing an Analysis of an Argument (p. 179)

Although we offer incidental comments about *writing* in Chapters 2 and 3—with comments on audience, tone, organization, and so on—this chapter and Chapter 6 contain our primary discussions of writing.

In Chapter 10, we reprint Carl R. Rogers's "Communication: Its Blocking and Its Facilitation," an essay that has interested many teachers of rhetoric because of its emphasis on psychological aspects of persuasion. The essay is fairly short and easy, and because it is mainly about a writer's interaction with an audience, it may well be assigned in conjunction with this chapter.

If you want to give a writing assignment *not* based on a reading assignment, this suggestion may be useful:

Write a letter (150–300 words) to the editor of a newspaper, responding to an editorial or to a published letter. Hand in the material you are responding to, along with your essay.

Nicholas D. Kristof

For Environmental Balance, Pick Up a Rifle (p. 186)

The student essay by Betsy Swinton, "Tracking Kristof," provides what we think is a thorough discussion of Kristof's essay. We in turn discuss Swinton's analysis, so we won't rehash the issue any further here.

Jeff Jacoby

Bring Back Flogging (p. 196)

Our society takes pretty much for granted that punishment for crimes will take the form of imprisonment, except for juveniles and first offenders, who may be offered probation instead. But the prison (as distinct from the jail, traditionally used only to detain accused persons prior to trial) is a relatively new invention in England and the United States, dating only from the end of the eighteenth century (see Michel Foucault, *Discipline and Punish: The Birth of the Prison* [1977], and Michael Ignatieff, *A Just Measure of Pain: The Penitentiary in the Industrial Revolution, 1750–1850* [1978]). Corporal punishments—the stocks, flogging, branding, mutilation, and hanging—are as old as recorded history, and some of these modes of punishment remain in use today, for example, in Saudi Arabia. Except for the death penalty, all such practices have been abandoned in the United States, and probably few would survive constitutional challenge were a legislature foolish enough to reintroduce them.

The case of flogging (or whipping) is different. Whipping survived in Delaware until 1952; in 1989, a bill was filed in the Delaware legislature to bring back the whipping post (see *New York Times*, January 29, 1989), but it failed to pass. It may come as a surprise to learn that the U.S. Supreme Court has yet to rule on the constitutionality of this classic mode of punishment. And for reasons Jeff Jacoby offers in his essay—inexpensiveness, brevity of duration, humiliation of offenders, and above all, physical pain—it retains a certain attractiveness in some quarters. Not until 1983, however, in the book *Just and Painful: A Case for the Corporal Punishment of Criminals* by criminologist Graeme Newman, did anyone in recent years seriously defend flogging. (Newman proposed electric shocks, carefully calibrated to suit the crime of the offender, followed by whipping if the offender recidivates, and incarceration only after repeated convictions for violent crimes.)

Our question 3 goes to the heart of the issue, as Jacoby realizes: Is it true that flogging (in whatever form and degree) is more degrading or brutal than imprisonment, and on that ground—entirely apart from any other consideration—ought to be abolished? Jacoby raises the issue and disposes of it with a rhetorical question ("where is it written, . . .?" para. 12). Flogging always brings to mind scenes of merciless beating; but such brutality is not necessary. It also often has overtones of sadistic pleasure aroused by the sight of naked flesh being turned to a bloody pulp; but, again, that is not necessary. Some opponents of flogging as punishment (including the authors of this manual) are repelled by the whole idea and cannot imagine ourselves inflicting such punishment on anyone, no matter what the crime, or of encouraging others to do it for us. But is this mere sentimentality, or is detesting such a practice a good enough reason for opposing it? Perhaps one can argue that when the abuses of imprisonment that Jacoby rightly reminds us of are compared with the abuses of flogging that Jacoby ignores, it is far from clear whether a reasonable and humane person ought to join him in preferring flogging.

Gerard Jones

Violent Media Is Good for Kids (p. 199)

First, we must confess that Jones's title irritates us: Pedants that we are, we wince when we see or hear *media* (from the Latin plural of *medium*) used as a singular noun. Still, we do understand that this usage is widely accepted, so we will grit our teeth and say only that we think "media is" sounds dreadful.

Jones's essay is not at all the sort of thing that most instructors want their students to write—it is essentially a personal essay—but it is devoted to a topic that has received a good deal of academic attention: the effect of imaginary violence on human beings. Probably the earliest extant major treatment of the issue in Western writing is Plato's denunciation of the poets in *The Republic*. The argument comes down to the idea that tragic and epic poets nourish the passions of their auditors, in other words stimulate human passions and therefore diminish human rationality. An almost comic version of this position appears in Boswell's *Life of Johnson*, where Boswell reports (September 23, 1777) a conversation with Johnson on the topic of the effect of music. Johnson told Boswell that music had little effect on him, and Boswell then reports his own responses to the power of music:

> I told him that [music] affected me to such a degree as often to agitate my nerves painfully, producing in my mind alternate sensations of pathetic dejection so that I was ready to shed tears, and of daring resolution, so that I was inclined to rush into the thickest part of the battle. "Sir," said he, "I should never hear it, if it made me such a fool."

Plenty of people agree that the arts stimulate passion, and that this is a Bad Thing. A common argument against pornography is that it stimulates unwholesome passions, and indeed plenty of sex offenders have said that they got their ideas (e.g., for bizarre forms of assault and murder) from films or books. On the other hand, one of the arguments offered in defense of pornography is that it may serve as a harmless release: The man who might otherwise rape a woman allegedly finds a release in a pornographic DVD.

The most famous defense of the depiction of antisocial emotions in literature is Aristotle's reply to Plato in the *Poetics*. Aristotle is talking about tragic drama in verse, but if what he says is true, it probably applies equally well to prose fiction. He says that when we perceive the artistic presentation of violence, we experience a *catharsis*. The trouble is, there is much argument about the exact meaning of *catharsis*. The basic Greek sense of the term is "purgation," in the medical sense—a laxative that purges the bowels. If something close to this is Aristotle's meaning, the idea is that we get rid of our emotions by experiencing them and discharging them harmlessly in the theater. It apparently is sort of like smashing a dish when one is angry; but do people really do this sort of thing, and if they do, does it work? That is, do the arts offer a sort of laxative for the emotions? We are back to the idea that porno allows the reader/viewer to get rid of unwholesome passions in a harmless way. But many scholars say that "purification" (or "cleansing") rather than "purgation" (or "discharge") is what Aristotle meant. Things get complicated here, but one version of this interpretation holds that by purification, Aristotle means that we see the *proper* objects of such emotions as pity and terror. For instance, when we witness a production of *King Lear*, we see an action that indeed evokes pity and terror, and we thus learn which kinds of actions should be pitied, and which kinds of actions are terrifying.

Some decades ago, Bruno Bettelheim, in *The Uses of Enchantment* (1976), argued that fairy tales that are filled with violence serve a wholesome purpose. In the story of "Hansel and Gretel," for example, there is a wicked witch, and the story ends with the children pushing the witch into an oven. Plenty of violence there. But, Bettelheim said, that's not bad. For one thing, he argued, such stories let children know that there are monstrous people in the world. Not everyone is a loving mother or father. Second, Bettelheim claimed, these stories serve to assure children that *their own* savage impulses are not unique, not aberrations, but are part of what all people have. That is, these stories serve the useful purpose of introducing children to the dark side of life. According to Bettelheim, children need to see that there are such impulses and need to learn how to handle them so that they may act maturely.

If you reread Jones's essay, you will hear plenty of Bettelheim. In the first paragraph Jones tells us that his parents insulated him from the real world of violence and that he "suffocated [his] deepest fears and desires under a nice-boy persona." In the fourth paragraph he tells us that he was "freed" by the image of the Hulk, who was an image of his own "stifled rage and buried desire for power." Jones claims to have seen something of his own history repeated in the life of his son. In the eleventh paragraph Jones says:

> Pretending to have superhuman powers helps children conquer the feelings of powerlessness that inevitably come with being so young and small.

We have not taught this essay, but we think that one good way to handle it is to ask students if parts or all of it rings true to their experience. They might then be asked to write an analysis of violence in media (or in one medium), drawing on their own experience but using a rather more academic style than Jones uses.

Justin Cronin

Confessions of a Liberal Gun Owner (p. 203)

We address, in sequence, the topics that we set forth in the book.

1. Cronin's title—rather than our imagined title of "Confessions of a Texas Gun Owner"—offers an engaging surprise. Gun owners in Texas presumably are not a rare species, but liberal gun owners are. In short, Cronin's title contains a hook, something that snares the reader's attention, whereas our invented alternative invites the response of "Ho hum, so what's new?"

2. Why so much autobiography? Because Cronin, in effect, is offering an essay based chiefly on one big—indeed, life-changing—experience, rather than an essay based largely on thinking analytically while sitting at desk, the sort of argumentative essay that would include statements such as "The three principle arguments in

favor of. . . ," and "On the other hand, we can counter the first of these arguments by offering two objections. . . ," and so forth.

3. Our view (based exclusively on our reading of the essay) is that Cronin is a very engaging guy, a good teacher, and a good colleague. He is earnest, clear, respectful of other ideas, and so on.

4. What *arguments* does he offer? Here, alas, we get uneasy. He does a good job of telling us how he came to feel the way he feels—but does he convince his readers that his position is sound? Because he does not much concern himself with setting forth and refuting opposing views, or offering anything in the way of statistics, we think that the skeptical reader probably remains skeptical. And there is a further problem: The life-changing experience that he reports (his decision to arm himself) is based on something that did *not* happen: He assures us (para. 11) that "chaos" would have occurred if the storm had hit Houston. But the storm did not hit Houston, and Cronin therefore cannot point to chaos—and the consequent need for a gun. Doubtless he could have called attention to other cities that have experienced looting, and these instances might have provided support for the argument that law-abiding folks need guns to protect their families—but he does not provide such evidence (e.g., statistics about looting after the flood in New Orleans), and we think this omission weakens his essay.

5. To this question (What would you say to a reader who told you that he or she didn't quite get Cronin's essay?) we offer no response—because, as we have just indicated, we are puzzled by Cronin's strategy of building an argument largely on something that did not happen. We will be interested in the responses of students.

6. Cronin in paragraph 13 sets forth his credentials as a liberal (he favors gun regulation, and he "loathes" the NRA), in effect reaffirming the strategy of his title and of his first paragraph. Still, it would have been interesting (and we think it would have been more convincing) if he had indicated exactly what sort of regulation he favors.

7. The comment that a short paragraph is usually an *underdeveloped* paragraph is true for analytic paragraphs (i.e., for most paragraphs in most argumentative essays) but of course is not true for some other kinds of paragraphs, and certainly not for all paragraphs in an essay that is largely biographical, as here, where Cronin reports the responses of a gun instructor and of his sixteen-year-old daughter. The paragraphs are especially effective partly *because* they are so short; they are packed with dynamite.

Peter Singer

Animal Liberation (p. 207)

This essay is an earlier version of text that became the opening chapter of Peter Singer's remarkably influential *Animal Liberation: A New Ethics for Our Treatment of Animals* (1975). In his book, Singer elaborates all his basic ideas, and especially "speciesism" (para. 18), to which he devotes a whole chapter.

Speciesism is the arbitrary favorable preference for members of our own species, and its logical consequence is an equally arbitrary but indifferent or hostile attitude toward lower species. Whether the analogy to racism, sexism, and other *-isms* is as instructive as Singer implies is another matter. In any case, he argues (para. 19) that the "case for Animal Liberation" does not depend on the analogy.

What, then, is animal liberation? Singer never says in so many words (see para. 3), but it amounts to, or at least can be stated as, a series of dos and don'ts: Don't kill animals to eat their flesh or to clothe your body, don't experiment on animals to save human lives or to reduce human misery, don't remove animals from their natural habitat. In short, don't treat animals as you would not like to be treated yourself.

Singer's opening paragraph is a model for the use of analogy to gain the high ground right from the start. Each of his readers will be able to identify with one or another of the groups he mentions that has been discriminated against in the past and so is immediately but unwittingly vulnerable to the "expansion of our moral horizons" about to unfold.

Singer worries (para. 12; our question 3) whether having intentions is necessarily, albeit mysteriously, connected with having the capacity to use language. We doubt that it is, and he does, too. Surely anyone who spends time with dogs and cats readily ascribes intentions to them ("He's trying to catch the stick when you throw it," "She's waiting to pounce on the mouse as soon as it moves"), and this use of intentional thinking is no more anthropomorphic than is ascribing intentions to other people. To insist that the latter is intelligible but the former isn't, because other people can speak a language whereas animals can't, pretty obviously begs the question. To insist that no creature can have an intention unless it can state what its intentions are is far too broad a thesis to defend; it would entail insisting that many human creatures do not have intentions, or act intentionally, when we believe they do. And so even if animals can't use language, because they lack the capacity, they may yet have minds enough to warrant a concern about how we intentionally treat them.

On what grounds does Singer base drawing the line where he does to demark the creatures that deserve our concern from those that don't? Why not draw the line elsewhere, particularly at the point that divides the living from the nonliving (not dead but inorganic or inert)? It wouldn't be at all satisfactory for Singer to answer: "Because I talk about creatures that can feel, and I don't about those that can't," although this reading seems to be true. But this can't be his answer because he does not want his argument to turn on who cares about what; he knows that most of us simply do not and will not easily come to care about animal welfare. A better line for him to take would be to refer to the *interests* of creatures and to the *equality* of their interests (para. 6), on the ground that only creatures with a capacity to suffer have interests, the first and foremost of which is to diminish their own suffering, pain, and discomfort. But on closer inspection, is it not still true that *all living* things have interests? Surely, a dogwood tree in the front yard has an interest in air, water, sunlight, and space to grow, even if it feels no pain when it is denied these things or when its leaves are plucked or—heaven forfend!—its branches slashed. To reason in this manner is to tie the concept of having an interest in something to the concept of something being good for a thing (water is surely good for a plant). But this is not what Singer does; rather, he ties a creature's interests to what it can feel. (See how he handles the case of the year-old infant in para. 15.)

When one goes in the other direction, as some have (for example, Christopher Stone, in *Should Trees Have Standing?* [1988]), a whole environmental ethic begins to unfold, but with alarming consequences, for even all but the most scrupulous vegetarian will neglect and even ruthlessly violate the interests of other living entities.

If we enlarge our moral community to include plants as well as animals—because all living entities have interests and because one interest is as good as another "from the point of view of the universe" (the criterion proposed by the utilitarian Henry Sidgwick, which Singer invokes in his *Animal Liberation*)—what will our moral principles permit us to eat? Not much, perhaps only unfruitful food, such as some of the surfeit of seeds and nuts produced by plants, and dead flesh, perhaps including even human flesh (our question 10). Killing to eat may be entirely ruled out, but eating what is dead isn't unless one appeals to some other moral principles besides the utilitarian notions Singer relies on.

This discussion can be put into an argument of this form: Because we have to eat to live, either we eat things that have interests or we don't. If we do, then we violate the equal interests of other creatures and thus act immorally. If we don't, then we can't kill living plants to eat them, any more than we can kill living animals to eat them. Instead, our survival depends on eating dropped fruit and seeds and carrion. Some readers will regard this argument as a reductio ad absurdum of Singer's position. Others will argue that it shows how difficult it is to formulate moral principles that we can really live by consistently and self-consciously.

Although persons who in journals debate with Singer often say that he subscribes to "animal rights," Singer has repeatedly denied that he believes that animals have "rights." Setting forth his disagreement with Tom Regan's *The Case for Animal Rights* (1983), Singer discusses the point at some length in the *New York Review of Books* (January 17, 1985, pp. 46–52). In a letter in the issue of April 25, 1985 (p. 57), he reaffirms his point. Singer explains that his view is utilitarian; he grants that conceivably there would be circumstances in which an experiment on an animal stands to reduce human suffering so much that it would be permissible to carry it out even if it involved some harm to the animal. (This would be true, he says in his letter of April 25, 1985, even if the animal were a human being.) In this letter he explains that, as a utilitarian, he advocates stopping animal experiments because

1. The suffering of an immense number of animals would be spared,

2. "The benefits lost would be uncertain," and

3. "The incentive thus provided for the speedy development of alternative methods of conducting research [would be] the most powerful imaginable."

Singer's essay, as we say in our headnote in the text, was first published in 1973 in the *New York Review of Books*. In the issue of May 15, 2003, Singer published, again in the *New York Review of Books,* "Animal Liberation at Thirty," a review of the state of the argument. His new essay makes special mention of the following books: Roger Scruton, *Animal Rights and Wrongs* (London: Metro, 1998); Paola Cavalieri, *The Animal Question: Why Non-human Animals Deserve Human Rights* (Oxford: Oxford University Press, 2001); David DeGrazia, *Taking Animals Seriously: Mental Life and Moral Status* (Cambridge: Cambridge University Press, 1996); Matthew Scully, *Dominion: The Power of Man, Suffering of Animals, and the Call to Mercy* (New York: St. Martin's, 2002).

We considered using the new piece instead of the first piece, but we finally decided that the first piece is much better for our use (the basic argument is set forward with few distractions), whereas in the recent piece Singer tries to take account of numerous questions and developments. But anyone — teacher or student — doing further work on this topic will want to consult the new essay.

Jonathan Swift

A Modest Proposal (p. 220)

Our discussion (p. 129) in these notes of Judy Brady's "I Want a Wife" offers a few general comments on satire, some of which are relevant to Jonathan Swift.

Unlike Brady's essay, where the title in conjunction with the author's name immediately alerts the reader that the essay cannot be taken straight, Swift's essay does not provide an obvious clue right away. In fact, some students don't perceive the irony until it is pointed out to them. Such imperceptiveness is entirely understandable. Swift's language is somewhat remote from twenty-first-century language, and in any case students don't expect satire in a collection of arguments. Moreover, it's hard today to know when a projector (the eighteenth-century name for someone with a bright idea) is kidding. A student who has not understood that "A Modest Proposal" is a satire may be extremely embarrassed upon learning the truth in public. To avoid this possibility, we usually begin the discussion by talking about Swift as a satirist who is known chiefly through *Gulliver's Travels,* and so on.

Most commentators on "A Modest Proposal" have concentrated on the persona of the speaker—his cool use of statistics, his way of regarding human beings as beasts ("a child just dropped from its dam" in para. 4, for example, or his reference to wives as "breeders" in para. 6), and, in short, his unawareness of the monstrosity of his plan to turn the children into "sound, useful members of the commonwealth" (para. 2), a plan that, by destroying children, will supposedly make the proposer "a preserver of the nation" (para. 2). Much of this complacent insensitivity and even craziness is apparent—on rereading—fairly early, as in the odd reference (para. 1) to "three, four, or six children" (what happened to five?), or, for that matter, in the phrases already quoted from paragraph 2. And of course it is true that one object of Swift's attack is the persona, a figure who, despite his profession that he is rational, practical, and compassionate, perhaps can be taken as an emblem of English indifference to Irish humanity. (But the speaker is an Irishman, not an Englishman.) More specifically, the leading object of attack can be said to be political reformers, especially those who heartlessly bring statistics ("I calculate," "I have reckoned," "I have already computed") where humane feelings should rule.

It is less often perceived, however, that the satire is also directed against the Irish themselves, with whom Swift was, by this time, fed up. *Satire* is almost too mild a word for the vehemence of "savage indignation" (Swift's own epitaph refers to his *saeva indignatio*) with which Swift denounces the Irish. Yes, he in effect says, the English treat the Irish abominably, but the Irish take no reasonable steps to help themselves. Even in so small a detail as the proposer's observation that his plan would cause husbands to stop beating pregnant wives (para. 26), we hear criticism not of the English but of the Irish. The chief denunciation of the Irish is evident, however, in the passage beginning with paragraph 29, in which Swift lists the "other expedients" that indeed the Irish themselves could (but do not) undertake to alleviate their plight.

In short, commentators who see Swift's essay simply as a scathing indictment of English hardheartedness are missing much of the point. One can almost go so far as to say that Swift's satire against the projector is directed not only against his impracticality and his unconscious cruelty but also against his folly in trying to help a nation that, out of stupidity and vanity, obstinately refuses to help itself. The projector sees the Irish as mere flesh; Swift at this time apparently saw them as something more exasperating, flesh that is stupid and vain. Swift was, we think, more than half in earnest when he had his crazy projector say, "I desire the reader will observe, that I calculate my remedy for this one individual kingdom of Ireland and for no other that was, is, or, I think ever can be upon earth."

If you wish students to do some research, you can ask them to look at Swift's "Irish Tracts" (*Prose Works*, ed. Herbert Davis, 12: 1–90, especially *Intelligencer* 19: 54–61), where they will find Swift arguing for the "other expedients" that his projector dismisses.

Related points:

1. This essay has ample material to demonstrate the use of the method that Aristotle calls "the ethical proof," that is, the pleader's use of his or her ethical character to persuade an audience. (Of course, here it backfires: We soon see a monster, not a benevolist.) Thus, in paragraph 1, the author shows his moral sensibility in using such expressions as "melancholy object" and "helpless infants." Also relevant is the projector's willingness to listen to other views—which he then of course always complacently rejects. (One might ask students to examine this issue through the eyes of Carl Rogers, who in his essay in Chapter 10 of the text urges writers to regard the views of the opposition sympathetically, not merely as points to be dismissed.)

2. A scattering of anti–Roman Catholic material (for example, references to "papists") indicates that the speaker, for all his insistence on his objectivity, is making a prejudiced appeal to emotions.

3. Instructors interested in satiric techniques will probably want to call attention to Swift's abundant use of diminution, such as people reduced to animals and to statistics.

Additional Topics for Critical Thinking and Writing

1. Drawing only on the first three paragraphs, write a brief characterization (probably three or four sentences) of the speaker—that is, of the persona whom Swift invents. Do not talk about Swift the author; talk only about the anonymous speaker of these three paragraphs. Support your assertions by quoting words or phrases from the paragraphs.

2. In an essay of 150–250 words, characterize the speaker of "A Modest Proposal," and explain how Swift creates this character. You may want to make use of your answer to the previous question, pointing out that at first we think such-and-such, but later, picking up clues that Swift provides, we begin to think thus-and-so. You may wish, also, to devote a few sentences to the last paragraph of Swift's essay.

3. What is the speaker arguing for? What is Swift arguing for?

4. Write a modest proposal of your own, suggesting a solution to some great social problem. Obvious topics include war, crime, and racism, but choose any topic that almost all people agree is a great evil. Do not choose a relatively controversial topic such as gay rights, vivisection, gun control, or right-to-work laws. Your proposed solution should be, like Swift's, outrageous, but your essay should not be silly. In the essay, you should satirize some identifiable way of thinking.

5. Following the same basic assignment as the previous one, this time write an essay on a topic that is controversial and about which you have strong feelings.

6
Developing an Argument of Your Own (p. 228)

In this chapter we try to help students get and develop ideas, chiefly by urging them (1) to ask themselves questions, (2) to write and rewrite, (3) to think of their audience as their collaborator, and (4) to submit drafts to peers for review. We think instructors will agree with us on the value of these practices. The trick is to convince students that even those who are pretty good writers will profit by working along these lines and, similarly, that even those who have difficulty writing *can* write interesting and effective papers if they make use of these suggestions.

All writers have their own methods of writing. Some can write only with a pen, whereas others can write only with a word processor; Balzac believed he needed the smell of rotten apples to stimulate his pen. Still, allowing for individual needs, we think it is honest to tell students that, in general, the sooner they begin an assignment, and the more they think about it and put their thoughts into notes and drafts, the better their essay will be. In an effort to make this point, we give in the text Emily Andrews's preliminary notes and second thoughts, as well as the final version of her essay.

Emily Andrews (student essay)

Why I Don't Spare "Spare Change" (p. 264)

As our comments in the text indicate, we think the essay is an effective piece of writing, but you may disagree, and you may want students to discuss its strengths and weaknesses and perhaps even to write a critical analysis or a response.

7
Using Sources (p. 267)

In our teaching, we try to inculcate the idea that the "research paper" is not a genre found only in the land of Freshman English or even in the larger realm of College Writing but is something that flourishes (under different descriptions, of course) wherever writing is required. That is, we try to help students to see that when, say, one writes a letter to a school newspaper, complaining that a coach has been fired, one first does (or ought to do) a little homework, finding out the won-lost record to strengthen the letter. And of course almost all reports written for businesses require research.

Students are more likely to work enthusiastically on their papers if they understand that using sources is an activity in which all literate people sometimes engage. In fact, students engage in research all the time, for instance, when they consult a book of baseball statistics or a catalog of recordings or when they talk with friends to find out what courses they should take next semester.

To give students some practice in finding materials (and in learning something), you might ask them to produce a bibliography of recent writings on, say, pornography, racist speech, or euthanasia, with summaries of two or three articles.

Part Three

FURTHER VIEWS ON ARGUMENT

8
A Philosopher's View:
The Toulmin Model (p. 337)

Of the many attempts by philosophers in recent decades to explain the logic of ordinary argumentation—and to do so in a manner that the general reader (especially undergraduates and faculty not trained in formal logic) can grasp—none has been as well received as the work of Stephen Toulmin. Toulmin began his career at Cambridge at the end of Ludwig Wittgenstein's tenure there as a professor and for many years was on the philosophy faculty of the University of Southern California.

Why Toulmin's model of argumentation should have proved so popular where others have failed is not entirely clear to us. No doubt his reputation as a philosopher among philosophers has helped; but that is hardly the whole story because few philosophers teach informal logic and fewer still use his book *The Uses of Argument* (1958, 1969) to do it. Surely his desire to avoid forcing every kind of argument into some version of an Aristotelian syllogism is attractive. Perhaps it is mostly that the six-step model he offers with its untechnical nomenclature ("claim," "ground," and so on) is relatively more user-friendly than what the competition has to offer. Whatever the explanation, we think instructors using this book, especially those making their first acquaintance with Toulmin's method here, will find it rewarding to study (if not also to teach).

James E. McWilliams

The Locavore Myth: Why Buying from Nearby Farmers Won't Save the Planet (p. 345)

If you assign this essay, you may want your students also to read the paired essays that constitute a debate in Chapter 16, The Local Food Movement: Is It a Better Way to Eat? They are Stephen Budiansky, "Math Lessons for Locavores," and Kerry Trueman, "The Myth of the Rabid Locavore."

9
A Logician's View:
Deduction, Induction, Fallacies (p. 349)

The purpose of this chapter is to develop at somewhat greater length the tools of reasoning introduced in Chapter 3. Here, in a few dozen pages, we divide the subject into three natural and familiar parts: deductive reasoning, inductive reasoning, and fallacious reasoning.

To take them in reverse order, we identify and illustrate eighteen fallacies. The list can be extended; for example, in the latest edition of his standard textbook, *With Good Reason*, 6th ed. (2004), S. Morris Engel identifies and discusses a dozen more. Few instructors will want to introduce their students to all the fallacies that we discuss; but we would hope that instructors would find it useful to dwell on a few from time to time. Here, we want to mention a popular fallacy (of the sort that logicians call "formal") that does not appear in our text or in Engel's textbook: the fallacy of *denying the antecedent*.

Consider this argument:

1. If it's raining, then the streets will be wet.

2. It isn't raining.

3. Therefore, the streets aren't wet.

This argument has the obvious form: if p then q; not p; therefore not q. The trouble is that this argument form is invalid; to see why, just consider the example above. Surely, it is possible the streets *are* wet—for example, a catch basin overflowed, the street cleaners flushed down the street—despite no rain at all. This argument is invalid because of its form, and we cannot trust any argument of this form. It has a related invalid argument form that is almost equally popular; its name is *affirming the consequent*, and this is its form: if p, then q; q; therefore, p. We leave it to your imagination to see why this form of argument is also invalid.

A large fraction (we cannot be more precise) of our daily reasoning is inductive, and to the few pages in Chapter 3 devoted to this topic we have added seven or eight more pages in this chapter. In the following pages, our aim is to take a couple of examples (involving fatality, or the risk thereof, caused by smoking) as the skeleton on which to hang our discussion of evidence, observation, inference, probability, confirmation, and related concepts essential to inductive reasoning. Brief though our discussion is, we think that at a minimum it should help instructors make these important concepts more accessible and usable by students and thus add to their available tools for diagnosing and constructing arguments.

Finally, we begin the chapter with a discussion of deduction, amplifying what we offered as a bare-bones introduction in Chapter 3. Here we offer another dozen terms (*dilemma, hypothetical syllogism,* and so on) that are standard vocabulary for the discussion of formal deductive reasoning. Some instructors may find it useful to work their way through our discussion with their students in class (perhaps in conjunction with the parallel material found in Chapter 3). Most instructors, we suspect, will find this material of use mainly for occasional reference. All (at least all instructors) can profit to greater or lesser degree merely by (carefully) reading these pages once over.

1. Abortion might be said to be a form of prenatal homicide—the killing of an unborn human being—but not murder, since the human embryo and fetus are months away from being a person. The fallacy is using a term (*murder*) that connotes the death of a person when no person is present in a prenatal homicide.

2. We think that it does matter whether the person in question is dying in any case, and whether he or she is suffering pain, especially pain that cannot be controlled by drugs.

3. The fallacy here is arguing for a general rule on the basis of a sample of one.

4. Invoking a right to listen whenever and to whatever you want is silly; the fallacy here is that there is no such right in the first place.

5. The comment suggests that it's better to be selfish and safe than altruistic at some personal risk. But is it really better? Better according to what standard or criterion? We side with the Good Samaritan, not with his selfish critic.

6. The epigram comes from American history out west in the 1870s. The fallacy here is tacitly recommending a violent course of action when dealing with strangers—or foreign nations—that is, assuming without any evidence that you cannot trust whoever knocks on your door.

7. There really isn't any fallacy here; the three generalizations are often invoked because they sum briefly the truth of the matter.

8. No fallacy here, either.

9. The fallacy here is inferring from dozens of suicide leaps off the bridge that there is no other or better way to prevent such acts than by closing the bridge down.

10. The fallacy here, from a practical point of view, is that there is little in common between the Japanese American claim for reparations and the current claim by African Americans for reparations. The Japanese American community in 1942 was well defined and relatively small in number, and calculating its losses was not an insuperable task. In all three respects, the situation with today's African Americans is different.

11. This is controversial, but we think that the statement is essentially correct. True, trees and stones do not bleed, whereas dogs and cats, as well as wild animals, do, and they also can feel pain. For some, following the lead of the great Jeremy Bentham, these feelings—pleasure and pain—are all that matters. One of us thinks otherwise. Human rights take their origin from the way they connect with distinctive capacities that only humans (so far) are known to have, chief among which is a sense of self. (The other of us has kept as many as four dogs at once. He holds a different view.)

12. The fallacy here is treating a mathematical average carried to one decimal point as though it were a whole number, in this case a number of children. For example, suppose there were 15 children whose ages sum to 45. The average age of the children is 45 divided by 15, or 3—a whole number. But suppose the ages of the 15 children sum to 42. Now the average is 2.8—not the number of children in any family.

13. The fallacy here is the same as the one we met in item 3.

14. It is possible to do as the Red Queen does, verdict first and evidence later. But you couldn't run a criminal justice system following this rule. The fallacy here is treating verdict and evidence as though the order or sequence in which they are carried out doesn't matter to the outcome of the trial, when of course it usually does. This rule violates a fundamental rule of criminal law, namely, that the accused has

a right to see the evidence being used against him, except after the trial is over, at which point giving the defendant access to the evidence against him is largely no longer of interest.

15. What counts as an "adequate reason" to believe that the moon has a back side when no such thing could be seen? Notice that the issue here is not whether the moon is spherical. Eclipses surely suggest that it has a circular (even if not spherical) shape. A spherical back side is surely a possibility. Since the issue is not whether you can rule out any particular shape for a back side, it seems reasonable to assume that the moon has some sort of back side, just as every three-dimensional object does.

16. The fallacy here is thinking of alcoholism as a highly likely outcome from steadily increasing the consumption of alcohol. It all depends on the dosage and the frequency. We can easily imagine cases of this sort; they turn on the volume and strength of the alcohol being imbibed. And because volume and frequency of consumption are relevant to the onset of alcoholism, we can equally imagine cases where no such addiction develops, because the dosage is small and the frequency moderate.

17. The big Indian is the mother of the little Indian.

18. This is the notorious gambler's fallacy, also known as the Monte Carlo fallacy. If you toss a coin fifteen times and each time the coin comes up heads, or comes up tails, or alternates heads and tails, you are probably dealing with some kind of unfair coin. If you toss a fair coin, the odds are 50-50 that it will come up heads. Since the heads-or-tails behavior of a fair coin has no effect on the *next* toss, the a priori probability of a coin coming up heads on the next toss is again 50-50, that is, identical to the a priori probability of the coin coming up tails. The fallacy is to think that the outcome of the current toss of a fair coin has some effect on the outcome of the next toss, and so on indefinitely, when it doesn't.

19. Well, in a lighthearted mood, one might agree; perhaps a bit of exercise each Sunday morning would be good for what ails one. But the reply of the loyal churchgoer will be that we have spiritual needs, too, and they cannot be served by walking or jogging. The fallacy, if there is one, is to think that physical needs are more important than spiritual ones, when a reasonable person might seek ways to satisfy both kinds of needs.

20. The fallacy here is ad hominem, acting as though a person's political affiliations govern all the beliefs and behavior of that person. Perhaps they do, but that is highly unlikely.

21. The fallacy here is post hoc, ergo propter hoc ("after this, therefore because of this"). For all we know, the terrorists have backed off, but not because our defense systems are so good. Perhaps they have run out of large sums of cash to buy weapons and finance attacks. Perhaps the supply of suicidal terrorists has declined. Perhaps they are thinking up new attacks that they will unleash in the next few weeks or months. And so on.

22. Well, just how reliable are press releases from the White House these days? Can we trust whatever they tell us? Surely, caution is advised. Pretty clearly, anyone who argues in this manner is committing the fallacy of appeal to authority, and also is arguing in a circle—offering as evidence the very issue that is to be proved. The statement comes down to this: You can trust them because they are trustworthy.

23. True, the theory of evolution so far cannot explain how life began. But perhaps in time it will, or perhaps some entirely new theory will supersede natural selection in the spirit of Darwin. In any case, it is an empirical question just how much Darwinism can explain. There is no reason to think that the failure, so far, of

natural selection to explain the origin of life is a reason for believing that intelligent design is the best or the only other explanation.

24. We are not devotees of Serrano's career, and we think the title he chose, *Piss Christ*, is in the worst possible taste. But there is no fallacy, certainly not any obvious one, on which to hang such a judgment. Given that the image (it is a photograph) exists (or did exist), we can imagine many who would like to see it if only to make a judgment of its worth for themselves. As for public funding, we are not deeply troubled by using a tiny portion of federal tax revenues to support the project; we do, however, find it difficult to see how Serrano's photograph could win out against any serious competition for public support. But let the panel of judges for such competitions decide on the merits.

25. We think the statement is true—but we would go further. Thomas should have expected more evidence before he believed his eyes. To settle the question in his mind—viz., is this man the resurrected Jesus of Nazareth, the Son of God—more evidence than a few scars on the man's body is required. After all, we are talking about one of the greatest miracle stories of western civilization, and it is difficult to overestimate the evidence it is reasonable to require. The fallacy, if any, lies in Thomas's willingness to believe on the strength of the slender evidence before him.

26. One way to read this narrative is to judge the baseball player guilty of the fallacy of post hoc, ergo propter hoc, which we have seen earlier in item 21.

27. This is an old Yankee saying, but it's not much of a dilemma. If it's a small hole, you could fix it in the rain, provided the rain is not too heavy. Better still, you could fix it on a day of good weather, knowing that it will rain sometime in the future, even if not soon, and that it's better to fix the hole than to leave it, even if doing so interrupts something you'd rather do, like working in the garden or watching the Patriots on their way to another Super Bowl victory. The fallacy here is thinking there is a serious dilemma when there isn't.

28. Because there's a better explanation. What we are witnessing is what sailors call a ship hull down on the horizon. The hull disappears from view as the ship moves steadily away from the pier (or shore) and at right angles to the beach (or shore), and so on with ever taller parts of the ship until the entire ship is lost to view. But no sinking is involved—though of course it might be involved. It's just very unlikely.

29. *Proves* in this familiar saying means "tests" (cf. the related noun, *proof*, when we speak of a photographic *proof* or when we say, "The proof of the pudding is in the eating"). Surely testing a rule by looking for exceptions is an important aspect of scientific reasoning. The fallacy lies in misunderstanding what *proves* means in this context.

30. Herbivores eat fruit and vegetable matter. Herbs such as oregano, thyme, rosemary, sage, and the rest do not form the diet of any herbivores, so far as we know. Perhaps the reason is that herbs tend to grow on small plants, whereas your standard herbivores—elephants, hippopotami—feast on large leaves.

31. First, the text of the ad is ambiguous. Does it mean "More doctors smoke Camels than smoke any other cigarette" or does it mean "More doctors smoke Camels than all the doctors who smoke other cigarettes plus all those who abstain from smoking"? The former version is probably what is meant. In any case, there is an appeal to authority implicit in the caption. Who am I to argue with doctors; if they prefer Camels, I should at least try a pack and see how I like them. Besides, if doctors prefer Camels, then surely these cigarettes must be safe to smoke whether or not others are equally safe. (All nonsense.)

32. Killing five to save one is absurd on its face—unless, of course, the five are hardened criminals and the one is a Nobel Prize–winning scientist. The really

tempting alternative is killing one to save five. This version violates the Kantian principle that one should never use a person as a means to serve the ends of other persons—in this case, the desire of the five to survive. Of course, if the one consents to being used by the five for their survival, that's another matter altogether. Morality respects sacrifice; it does not demand it. We cannot lodge a complaint if no one volunteers to be sacrificed. If the right to life means anything at all, it means that the many have no right to take the life of the one, since to do so violates the right to life of the one. There is, of course, much more to be said. Some of that more can be found in the slender volume by Hugo Bedau, *Making Mortal Choices: Three Exercises in Moral Casuistry* (1997).

Max Shulman

Love Is a Fallacy (p. 383)

There are lots of laughs here, but the piece *does* teach effectively; students are more likely to remember Max Shulman's discussion of fallacies than ours. One can also use the story—especially the first paragraph—to talk about style. Read the first sentence aloud in class ("Cool was I and logical") and ask students what sorts of expectations are set up. Most will see that he *must* be kidding. And so on through the paragraph, to "And—think of it!—I was only eighteen."

We urge you to assign this story.

10

A Psychologist's View:
Rogerian Argument (p. 392)

Carl R. Rogers

Communication: Its Blocking and Its Facilitation (p. 394)

An occasional student has told us that Carl R. Rogers is "merely trying to apply psychology" to outwit his opponent, but we believe this interpretation is mistaken. Rogers was much concerned with reducing tension so that issues could be more easily discussed, not with deceiving the parties involved. Still, it is easy to see how students might think that "psychology" is a weapon to be wielded—something akin to bluffing at poker—in order to win. We are reminded of the advice that an old actor gave to a young one: "The most important thing is sincerity. When you can fake *that*, you can do anything."

It's not hard to find comments about argument that come close to the actor's view. Consider, for instance, Samuel Butler's "It is not he who gains the exact point in dispute who scores most in controversy, but he who has shown the most forbearance and the better temper." Or Lord Chesterfield's advice to his son: "If you would convince others, seem open to conviction yourself." But Butler's concern with scoring most and Chesterfield's use of *seem* (as opposed to *be*) set their comments sharply apart from Rogers's. Similarly, consider Ben Franklin: "Those disputing, contradicting, and confuting people are generally unfortunate in their affairs. They get victory, sometimes, but they never get good will, which be of more use to them." Rogers would probably agree, but he would rightly claim that he is not concerned with gaining goodwill so that it will be of "use" to him; he is concerned with helping the world to achieve peace.

Much closer to Rogers than Butler, Chesterfield, or Franklin is Pascal: "When we wish to correct with advantage, and to show another that he errs, we must notice from what side he views the matter, for on that side it is usually true." Close—but still short of Rogers's view, since Rogers recognizes that the other side not only may be right from its own point of view but may indeed be right enough so that we can come to accept at least part of that point of view. Consider these key statements:

> The whole task of psychotherapy is the task of dealing with a failure in communication. (para. 1)

> If you really understand another person in this way, if you are willing to enter his private world and see the way life appears to him, without any attempt to make evaluative judgments, you run the risk of being changed yourself. You might see it his way, you might find yourself influenced in your attitudes or your personality. (para. 11)

We imagine that most people would agree with Rogers in theory, but some opposing voices have been heard. For us, the most telling objection is that Rogers speaks as a white male—that is, as a member of the group that for centuries has done most of the speaking and has done very little listening. His advice—in effect, "Calm down, listen to me, and see things from my point of view"—is good advice for people like Rogers but is less useful (we have heard it said) for women, gays and lesbians, blacks, Hispanics, and other marginalized people. Some members of these groups say that they have listened long enough, and that it is now their turn to speak out and to speak out forcefully. Let straight white males, they argue, do the listening for a change.

One other point must be made about Rogerian argument. Rogers was talking about *talking,* about people who are actually facing their hearers. But instructors who use our book are for the most part concerned with *writing,* and they may wonder if Rogers's essay is relevant to writers. We offer two short answers: (1) Assign and discuss the essay, and (2) urge students to make use of the checklist in the text (p. 400) when they write their next essays. We think that if students read the essay and pay attention to the checklist, they not only will write better essays but also may become better people.

Edward O. Wilson

Letter to a Southern Baptist Minister (p. 400)

When students read an essay, they are inevitably concerned chiefly with the content of the argument rather than with the essayist's strategies, but here and there in our text we urge students to study an essayist's *ways* of arguing. That is, we urge them to see how the writer is conducting the argument. We give Wilson's essay in this chapter not because we are especially concerned with his views of God or, for that matter, of nature, but because we want students to see how he goes about talking to—well, we can put it bluntly—the opposition. And this will be our concern here.

The opening paragraph in effect offers a warm, hearty handshake. In the very first sentence Wilson says, "I feel I know you well enough to call you friend." In the second sentence he says that "we grew up in the same faith," and in the third he is a bit more specific: "I went under the water." In other words, Wilson, like the pastor whom he addresses, was baptized. (Not all students will understand "I went under the water.") In the fourth sentence he confesses that he no longer is a believer, but in this very sentence he goes on to express confidence that if he and his reader speak of their "deepest beliefs," it will be "in a spirit of mutual respect and good will." After all, he goes on to say, assuring his reader, not only are they both Americans but they are Southerners, people who share a code of "civility and good manners." Wilson has certainly made every effort to ingratiate himself. Only the most churlish reader would refuse to listen to what Wilson has to say.

Paragraph 2: Wilson begins, "I write to you now for your counsel and help." Well, what reader (or listener) would refuse to offer advice and help to this nice man who says he needs our assistance? Wilson then goes on to sketch his reader's central views.

Paragraph 3: Wilson begins, by way of contrast, with a sketch of his own views, which of course differ sharply from his supposed auditor's.

Paragraph 5: Wilson asserts that the "difference in worldview" does not separate the two men in all things, and he goes on to say that both of them value "security, freedom of choice, personal dignity, and a cause to believe in that is larger than ourselves." This last belief is especially important: "A cause . . . that is larger than ourselves" has a vaguely religious sound that is not present in "freedom of choice."

Paragraph 6: The paragraph begins, "Let us see, then, if we can, and you are willing, to meet." Again we hear the earnest expression of a desire to share, to work things out courteously.

Paragraph 7: After "Pastor, we need your help," Wilson says, "The Creation—living Nature—is in deep trouble." Notice—and we think this is very important—that Wilson uses a capital letter for "Creation." We think the use of a capital is important because it is our guess that his auditor might use a capital letter in speaking of "the Creator." That is, Wilson is doing all that he possibly can do to establish common ground, to speak the language of his auditor.

It would be very easy to proceed through the essay in this fashion, but it is unnecessary; so let's jump to paragraph 14, which Wilson begins thus:

> To make the point in good Gospel manner, let me tell the story of a young man newly trained for the ministry, and so fixed in his Christian faith that he referred all questions of morality to readings from the Bible.

Again, in his reference to "good Gospel manner," Wilson reminds us that he was brought up as a churchgoer—remember, in his first paragraph he said that he "went under the water"—and he then goes on to offer the surprising information that the young man of the story was Charles Darwin, in 1832. The next paragraph quotes from Darwin in 1859, speaking of "grandeur," and of something "breathed into a few forms or into one." We take it that Darwin's "breathed into" evokes Genesis 2:7, "And the Lord God formed man of the dust of the ground, and breathed into his nostrils the breath of life. And man became a living soul." Darwin was doing his best to imply that his vision had its affinities with the Judeo-Christian vision, and that's what Wilson is also doing, for instance, in his seventeenth paragraph, where he speaks of Darwin's "*reverence* (emphasis ours) for life."

The essay concludes with the assertion that Wilson and his Christian reader "have a common purpose," at least concerning the "life-and-death issue" of the future of the planet. It's all very Rogerian.

11
A Rhetorician's View: Rhetorical Analysis of Nontraditional Texts (p. 404)

Unfortunately, today in ordinary speech, the word *rhetoric* is chiefly used with negative connotations, in such phrases as "empty rhetoric," "mere rhetoric," and "rhetoric, not action." On the other hand, criticism of rhetoric is hardly new: In ancient times, Plato criticized the Sophists for pretty much the same reason that some people today criticize "rhetoric," that is, that it allegedly is divorced from truth and is used chiefly for deceptive purposes.

The high view of rhetoric of course is very different: It is (as we several times say in the text) both (1) an *instrument for discovering truth* and then (2) an instrument for propagating the truth by means of persuasive devices, and thus it is an art or a skill that every responsible citizen should possess. As teachers of argumentative writing, we subscribe to this high view.

Here are two quotations affirming the high value of rhetoric:

Histories make men wise; poets, witty; the mathematics, subtle; natural philosophy, deep, moral, grave; logic and rhetoric, able to contend.

Francis Bacon (1561–1626)

The design of Rhetoric is to remove those Prejudices that lie in the way of Truth; to Reduce the Passions to the Government of Reasons; to place our Subject in a Right Light, and excite our Hearers to a due consideration of it.

Mary Astell (1666–1731)

This chapter is especially concerned with providing students with tools that enable them to analyze twenty-first-century forms of argument, for example, electronic communications.

12
A Literary Critic's View:
Arguing about Literature (p. 420)

Classroom discussion usually centers on the meaning of a work, and almost always some-one raises the question, "Do you really think that's what the author intended?" But ever since the publication of W. K. Wimsatt Jr. and Monroe C. Beardsley's "The Intentional Fallacy," *Sewanee Review* 54 (Summer 1946), conveniently reprinted in W. K. Wimsatt Jr.'s *The Verbal Icon* (1954), it has been impossible (we think) to talk easily about the author's intention.

To begin with, most authors have not in any explicit way set forth their inten-tions: We have, for example, *Hamlet,* but not Shakespeare's comment on his intention in the drama. Nevertheless, students may say that if an author has stated what he or she intended, we should interpret the work accordingly. But we might respectfully point out that the stated intention is not always fulfilled in the work. The author doubtless intended to write a great work—but does this intention mean that the work is great? The author intended to write a serious work—but we may find it absurd. Does the author's intention make the work less absurd? Or, conversely, the writer may have intended only to earn money. A famous instance is Dr. Johnson, hurriedly writing *Rasselas* to pay the costs of his mother's funeral but nevertheless producing a masterpiece. Wimsatt and Beardsley have taught us that the work "means" what the work itself says, not what the author says he or she meant it to mean. In the words of Lillian Hellman, "The writer's intention hasn't anything to do with what he achieves." Or in the words of D. H. Lawrence, "Never trust the artist. Trust the tale."

Although "The Intentional Fallacy" remains the classic text, you may want to suggest that students interested in this topic should read Beardsley's later comments on inten-tion in his *Aesthetics: Problems in the Philosophy of Criticism* (1958) and in his *The Possibility of Criticism* (1970).

The proper question to ask, we believe, is not "What did the author mean?" but, rather, "What does the text say?" We can, of course, try to see what the work meant in its own day—that is, in its historical context. For instance, if we are thinking about *The Merchant of Venice* or about *Othello,* we can try to collect information about Elizabethan atti-tudes toward Jews or toward Moors, respectively, but even with such material, we will not be able to say much about Shakespeare's intention. *The Merchant of Venice* contains at least one extended passage (3.1.55–65) in which Shylock is presented far more sympathetically than any Jew in any other Elizabethan text (Did Shakespeare perhaps find Shylock coming to life, and did he give him better lines than he intended?). As for *Othello,* well, no other Elizabethan drama has a tragic hero who is a Moor. The mere fact that Shakespeare alone made a Moor the central figure in a tragedy—a genre that displayed human greatness— suggests that we will not get much insight into Othello by seeing how other dramatists represented Moors or, for that matter, even by seeing how Shakespeare represented Moors in other plays (*Titus Andronicus* and *The Merchant of Venice*). To read *Othello* is to see a Moor who is incontestably different from the Moors in all other Elizabethan plays (including Shakespeare's other plays), and we do great injustice to the heroic Othello if we push him into the mold of "the Elizabethan Moor," which in effect means the Moor as depicted by people who were not Shakespeare.

Let's take a particular passage in T. S. Eliot's "The Love Song of J. Alfred Prufrock" (Chapter 27). After the epigraph from Dante, the poem begins thus: "Let us go then, you and I." Who is the "you"? In this manual we suggest that "Prufrock" is an internal monologue in which the timid self ("I") addresses his own amorous self as "you." (We don't say that *every* "you" in the poem is the amorous self.) It happens that a reader asked Eliot (apparently in the mid-1940s, some thirty years after Eliot wrote the poem) who the "you" is, and Eliot replied:

> As for THE LOVE SONG OF J. ALFRED PRUFROCK anything I say now must be somewhat conjectural, as it was written so long ago that my memory may deceive me; but I am pre-pared to assert that the "you" in THE LOVE SONG is merely some friend or companion, presumably of the male sex, whom the speaker is at that moment addressing. . . .

> (Kristian Smidt, *Poetry and Belief in the Work of T. S. Eliot,* 85.)

Several points are worth noting: (1) The statement was made long after the poem was written, and Eliot grants that any such late statement "must be somewhat conjectural"; (2) he nevertheless is "prepared to assert" that the "you" is "some friend or companion"; (3) although he is prepared to make this assertion, the assertion itself is rather imprecise (there is a difference between a "friend" and a "companion") and he immediately goes on to reveal (by saying "presumably of the male sex") that he himself no longer has (if he ever did have) a clear idea of who the "you" is. How helpful, then, is his comment? True, if one wants to say that the author is the decisive authority, presumably one can rule out the view that the "you" in the poem is (for the most part) the amorous self, the self urg-ing the timid self to go forward. But, we suggest, the test is to read the poem to see if the suggestion makes sense.

Eliot himself occasionally commented at some length on the topic of intention. For instance, in "The Social Function of Poetry" (1945) after saying that "a great deal more goes to the making of poetry than the conscious purpose of the poet," he went on to add, "And in recent times, a reason why we have become more cautious in accepting a poet's expressed intention as evidence of what he was really doing, is that we have all become more conscious of the role of the unconscious." And in "The Frontiers of Criticism" (1956) he mentions, of a published interpretation of "Prufrock" that he had recently read, "[The author set forth] an attempt to find out what the poem really meant—whether that was what I had meant it to mean or not. And for that I was grateful." Possibly Eliot's expres-sion of gratitude is spoken with tongue in cheek (though we do not think so), but even if one does think Eliot is being ironic, the case for the authority of the author's interpreta-tion is undermined; the author may (or may not) be speaking ironically, so how much weight can we give to his comments? In any case, in the context of the entire essay, it is clear that Eliot really does believe that a work cannot be reduced to what the author "intended."

One last quotation from Eliot, this one from *The Use of Poetry and the Use of Criticism* (1933, 130):

> A poet can try, of course, to give an honest report of the way in which he himself writes: the result may, if he is a good observer, be illuminating. And in one sense, but a very lim-ited one, he knows better what his poems "mean" than can anyone else; he may know the history of their composition, the material which has gone in and come out in an unrecog-nisable form, and he knows what he was trying to do and what he was meaning to mean. But what a poem means is as much what it means to others as what it means to the author; and indeed, in the course of time a poet may become merely a reader in respect to his own works, forgetting his original meaning.

These sentences make sense, but we also see the force of the commonsense view that a competent author shapes the material so that it embodies his or her meaning. This mean-ing may change during the process of composition—the writer finds his or her intention shifting and therefore revises the work—but, in this view, the creator of a work does know, at the end, what the meaning of the work is. Notice that we say "a competent author." Obviously an incompetent author may compose a work that is inadvertently incoherent or ludicrous and be unaware of the result. But a competent author, in this view, shapes the work—admittedly modifying the original intention as the work proceeds—and at the end has produced a work in which all of the elements cohere and on whose meaning he or she can comment. This, we say, is a commonsense view; the only trouble, again, is that most writers have not commented on their works (for example, Chaucer, Shakespeare), and those writers who have commented (for example, Eliot) have often made inconclusive remarks. Aside from Eliot, none of the poets, story writers, or dramatists represented in this book have commented on the works we reprint.

Robert Frost

Mending Wall (p. 426)

Some critics applaud the neighbor in Robert Frost's "Mending Wall," valuing his respect for barriers. For an extreme version, see Robert Hunting, "Who Needs Mending?" *Western Humanities Review,* 17 (Winter 1963: 88–89). The gist of this faction is that the neighbor wisely realizes—as the speaker does not—that individual identity depends on respect for boundaries. Such a view sees the poem as a Browningesque dramatic monologue like "My Last Duchess," in which the self-satisfied speaker unknowingly gives himself away.

Richard Poirier, in *Robert Frost* (1977), makes the interesting point that it is not the neighbor (who believes that "good fences make good neighbors") who initiates the ritual of mending the wall; rather, it is the speaker: "I let my neighbor know beyond the hill." Poirier suggests that "if fences do not 'make good neighbors,' the making of fences can," for it makes for talk—even though the neighbor is hopelessly taciturn. For a long, judicious discussion of the poem, see John C. Kemp, *Robert Frost: The Poet as Regionalist* (1979, 13–25).

Andrew Marvell

To His Coy Mistress (p. 435)

First, we touch on our final question, the emendation of "glew" to "dew" in line 34. This emendation has found wide acceptance, but the original reading may be right, not in the ordinary sense of glue, of course, but in a sense that H. Grierson suggested, "a shining gum found on some trees."

Probably most of the discussion in class will concentrate on the structure of the poem and the question of whether the poem is offensively sexist. As for the tripartite structure, which we call attention to in a question in the text, we want to make two points here. First, we do not see it as a Hegelian matter of thesis/antithesis/synthesis, although many readers do see it this way. We see it, as we indicate in the text, as a matter of a supposition, a refutation, and a deduction.

The supposition is somewhat comic, with the lover offering to devote two hundred years to the praise of each breast, and it is even somewhat bawdy in his offer to devote "thirty thousand to the rest": After all, what can "the rest" be, after he has praised her forehead, eyes, and breasts? This apparently leisurely state might, at first thought, seem to be ideal for a lover, but when one thinks about it, one perceives its barrenness: "We would sit down, and think which way / To walk, and pass our long love's day" (lines 3–4). Nothing is fulfilled: "An age at least to every part, / And the last age should show your heart" (lines 17–18), which is to say that after centuries of praising this or that part, the last age—an unimaginably long period—would be devoted to praising the countless good qualities of her heart, for instance her generosity, kindness, piety, and whatever else. It all sounds rather barren.

The second unit begins with lines that are among the most famous in English literature: "But at my back I always hear / Time's wingèd chariot hurrying near" (lines 21–22). These lines seem to introduce swiftness and vitality into the poem; but when one comes to think further about this unit, one notices that, at least so far as the man and the woman are concerned, they don't do much here either. In the "deserts of vast eternity," her beauty will *not* be found; his song will *not* be heard; they will not embrace. The chief actors will be the worms, who will "try" her virginity. If in the first unit the speaker spoofs the woman, showing her as a caricature of the disdainful mistress, in the second unit he savagely attacks her verbally, with talk of graves and worms. And here, too, as we have just said, nothing much happens.

In the third unit, there is plenty of (imagined) action, action that they share, unlike the earlier action of the speaker praising the beloved or of her refusing his offers. This joint action, sexual union, is indicated by "we," "us," and "our." But the imagery and the emotion are not what we might have expected. The savagery persists, notably in the images of "fire" and "birds of prey" (rather than the doves of Venus, which we might expect in a love poem) and in the verbs "devour" and "tear." Instead of time devouring the lovers, they devour time, but now we feel that the speaker's assertions lacerate himself as well as the beloved.

This gets us to our main point: We see the poem not so much as primarily a love poem or even as a poem of seduction (which is what disturbs many students), but as primarily a poem about the desperate condition of human beings, as the speaker sees it. To this extent, what interests a reader (we think) is the emotional states through which the speaker moves, from teasing the beloved (the first unit), to twisting the knife (the second unit), to forcing himself to face the facts that he has been thrusting under her eyes (the third unit).

Kate Chopin

The Story of an Hour (p. 438)

The first sentence of Kate Chopin's story, of course, proves to be essential to the end, though during the middle of the story, the initial care to protect Mrs. Mallard from the "sad message" seems almost comic. Students may assume, too easily, that Mrs. Mallard's "storm of grief" is hypocritical. They may not notice that the renewal after the first shock is stimulated by the renewal of life around her ("the tops of trees . . . were all aquiver with the new spring of life") and that before she achieves a new life, Mrs. Mallard first goes through a sort of death and then tries to resist renewal: Her expression "indicated a suspension of intelligent thought," she felt something "creeping out of the sky," and she tried to "beat it back with her will," but she soon finds herself "drinking in a very elixir of life through that open window," and her thoughts turn to "spring days, and summer days."

Implicit in the story is the idea that her life as a wife—which she had thought was happy—was in fact a life of repression or subjugation, and the awareness comes to her only at this late stage. The story has two surprises: The change from grief to joy proves not to be the whole story, for we get the second surprise, the husband's return and Mrs. Mallard's death. The last line ("the doctors . . . said she had died . . . of joy that kills") is doubly ironic: The doctors wrongly assume that she was overjoyed to find that her husband was alive, but they were not wholly wrong in guessing that her last day of life brought her great joy.

In a sense, moreover, the doctors are right (though not in the sense they mean) in saying that she "died of heart disease." That is, if we take the "heart" in a metaphorical sense to refer to love and marriage, we can say that the loss of her new freedom from her marriage is unbearable. This is not to say (though many students do say it) that her marriage was miserable. The text explicitly says "she had loved him—sometimes." The previous paragraph in the story nicely calls attention to certain aspects of love—a satisfying giving of the self—and yet also to a most unpleasant yielding to force: "There would be no one to live for her during those coming years; she would live for herself. There would be no powerful will bending her in that blind persistence with which men and women believe they have a right to impose a private will upon a fellow creature."

A biographical observation: Chopin's husband died in 1882, and her mother died in 1885. In 1894, in an entry in her diary, she connected the two losses with her growth. "If it were possible for my husband and my mother to come back to earth, I feel that I would unhesitatingly give up every thing that has come into my life since they left it and join my existence again with theirs. To do that, I would have to forget the past ten years of my growth—my real growth."

Having said what we have to say about the story, we now offer our own responses to the critical assertions in the text to which we ask students to respond.

1. We don't think the railroad accident is a symbol of the destructiveness of the Industrial Revolution. In our view, something in a text becomes symbolic by virtue of being emphasized, perhaps by being presented at considerable length or perhaps by being repeated at intervals. Nothing in the story connects the train with the Industrial Revolution; it is not, for instance, said to have altered the landscape, changing what was once an agrarian community into an industrial community. On the other hand, we think that in this story the coming of spring is symbolic of new life. Why? For one thing, Chopin explicitly says in the fifth paragraph that the "tops of trees . . . were all aquiver with the new spring life." She goes on to talk of "the delicious breath of rain" and of sparrows twittering. The rain of course is refreshing, and it is a fact that water brings about renewed life. Further, literary tradition (cf. Chaucer's reference to April showers at the start of *The Canterbury Tales*) has given spring showers a symbolic meaning. Sparrows are associated with sexuality (the sparrow is an attribute of Aphrodite), but we don't usually bring this up in class because Chopin mentions the sparrows only briefly and because students are not likely to know of the tradition. (This point seems to us not worth arguing.) A few paragraphs later Chopin tells us that something was coming toward Mrs. Mallard "out of the sky, reaching toward her through the sounds, the scents, the color that filled the air." Surely, therefore, it is reasonable to say that Chopin is emphasizing the season—its sounds, scents, and colors. A few paragraphs later, Chopin tells us that Mrs. Mallard was thinking of "spring days, summer days." In short, *in the story* spring is given an emphasis that the train is not, and so we tend to think that the spring is not just the spring but is something more, something whose implications we should attend to.

2. To say that the story claims that women rejoice in the deaths of their husbands seems to us to be a gross overgeneralization. The story is about one particular woman. True, in reading any work we may find ourselves saying, "Yes, life is sometimes like that," or some such thing. But nothing in the story suggests that it is about "women," and certainly nothing suggests that Mrs. Mallard's response toward the death of her husband is *typical* of "women."

3. The view that her death at the end of the story is a just punishment strikes us as going far beyond the text; we find no evidence that Chopin judges Mrs. Mallard harshly, and we think we can point to contrary evidence—for instance, to the sympathetic way in which her response is set forth.

5. We do not agree that the story is good *because* it has a surprise ending—but we also do not condemn it because of the ending. True, some critics would argue that surprise endings are tricks, that such endings are far less important than plausible characters, and so on. Our own view is that if a story offers virtually nothing but a surprise ending, it is probably a weak story—one can hardly read it a second time with any interest—but a certain amount of surprise surely is desirable. Most, maybe all, realistic prose fiction makes use of foreshadowing; expectations are set up, but they are fulfilled in slightly unexpected ways. We are reminded of a passage in E. M. Forster's *Aspects of the Novel* (1927):

> Shock, followed by the feeling, "Oh, that's all right," is a sign that all is well with plot: characters, to be real, ought to run smoothly, but a plot ought to cause surprise.

Of course one might argue that this view is arbitrary; here is a chance to ask students what values they might establish—what makes them say that a story is good or bad or so-so.

Plato

"The Greater Part of the Stories Current Today We Shall Have to Reject" (p. 443)

This excerpt from Plato's *Republic* is a passage near the end of Book II, in which Socrates undertakes to describe the proper education for that handful of the young intended to become the guardians or rulers of the ideal state. (Throughout the dialogue, we hear nothing about how the rest of the population is to be educated, that presumably being a matter of no interest.) After explaining the importance of "gymnastics," or bodily training, Socrates turns to "music," or training for the soul. To be fair, one must not take Platonic-Socratic admonitions out of context; nevertheless, there is some reason to believe that— unlike Socrates, who relied on the free air of Athens to carry out his ideas about education of the citizenry—Plato, the son of an Athenian nobleman, really did believe that a stricter regimen involving some censorship of the prevailing methods was appropriate.

Plato's argument for discarding the Homeric tales about the gods depends on accepting the principle that whatever is good can be the cause only of good things—hence the gods, being wholly good, cannot cause any of the bad things that the prevailing mythology attributes to them. Plato knows that the gods are wholly good only because that is part of his implicit definition of deity—as though he had said, "I [we?] wouldn't call it divine unless it was (morally) good."

Plato even goes so far as to allege that in his ideal state, it would be "sinful, inexpedient, and inconsistent" to permit the poets to say that "those who were punished were made wretched through god's action." Presumably, he thinks it would be inconsistent to allow this statement (question 3) because it would contradict something that the elder guardian-teachers themselves avow: namely, that (as Plato says at the end of the excerpt) "God is the cause, not of all things, but only of good." Thus when a poet presents a story in which a god is depicted as making a person "wretched" (and we assume that being made wretched is not a "good" thing, but that getting your deserved punishment is), this interpretation contradicts the doctrine above because it makes the god out to be the cause of something not "good."

Some will complain that Plato assumes, on no explicit evidence, that "children cannot distinguish between what is allegory and what isn't," and he shows throughout that he underestimates the capacity of children to distinguish the silly from the serious, the cheap from the dear, and the obscene from the respectful (our question 2). It is, of course, an empirical question—and not an easy one to answer—whether children can make these distinctions. But it is needless to speculate whether they can make them in the abstract or in a wholly nonsocial environment. As we remember our childhood and that of our friends, we testify that we had no great difficulty in making these distinctions and that an unremitting diet of Saturday afternoon B-grade films at the local movie palace or the standard TV fare of the 1950s did not hopelessly muddle our values and our sense of reality. Obviously, we did not feed only on such stuff, any more than children today see nothing except what is on the most violent television shows. Even if we overestimate our own ability as youngsters to sort the wheat from the chaff, we doubt that the best way to develop judgment about what is harmful, tasteless, offensive, and worse is to deny all access to the meretricious, salacious, and blasphemous. Even if this is too serene (or radical) a view to gain favor, one must eventually face the question *quis custodiet custodies,* or "Who shall guard the guardians?" Plato does not need to worry about this problem because he, unlike the rest of us, deals by definition with an ideal state and its appropriately ideal government, one that is incapable of the provinciality of every known board of public censorship.

13
A Debater's View: Individual Oral Presentations and Debate (p. 450)

If you require students to engage in formal debates, you may want to put a few books on reserve in the library. We especially recommend Bill Hill and Richard W. Leeman, *The Art and Practice of Argumentation and Debate* (1997). Also of some use are Jon M. Ericson, James J. Murphy, and Raymond Bud Zeuschner, *The Debater's Guide*, 3rd ed. (2003), and Leslie Phillips, William S. Hicks, and Douglas R. Springer, *Basic Debate*, 4th ed. (1996).

If you don't use formal debates but you do ask students to make oral presentations, we think you may still suggest that students read this chapter, paying special attention to the checklist. And you may want to emphasize these four points:

1. Provide transitions, such as *In the first place, further,* and *finally.*

2. Summarize occasionally, especially as you move from one point to the next.

3. Have a pretty full outline, and don't hesitate to glance at it occasionally while speaking, but do not read your speech.

4. As a listener, be courteous (no eye-rolling).

Part Four

CURRENT ISSUES: OCCASIONS FOR DEBATE

SOME THOUGHTS ABOUT ARGUMENT, ESPECIALLY ABOUT DEBATES AND BINARY THINKING

Anyone who has read the prefaces to a few recent texts on argument will have noticed that most of them disparage the idea that an argument is essentially a conflict, the presentation of a thesis with material that is intended to refute countertheses. These prefaces are quite different from those of an older generation, in which students were taught how to "marshall" evidence, how to "attack" the weak points in an "opponent's" argument, how to "defend" their own position, and, in short, how to "win" an argument. Thus we teachers of composition were given textbooks with militant titles such as *Point Counter-Point* and *Crossfire*. Today it is regularly said—and we ourselves say this in our text and in the classroom—that an argument is an effort to get at the truth, an endeavor in which those who hold other views are our fellow workers, helping us to refine our ideas, with the ultimate goal of arriving at a position that reasonable folks can agree on. This is especially evident in the Toulmin method, where the claim, the grounds, and the warrant all converge on the truth. (It is a sign of the times that the textbook formerly called *Crossfire* has been reissued with a new title, *Dialogues*.) In the preface to our text, and then again later in the text, we quote two passages, one by Edmund Burke and one by John Stuart Mill, that are constantly in our minds, and that we believe ring true to our experience. Here yet again are the passages:

> He that wrestles with us strengthens our nerves, and sharpens our skill. Our antagonist is our helper. (Burke)

> He who knows only his own side of the case knows little. (Mill).

Both of these passages imply, however faintly, that after careful thought, with the help of a worthy antagonist, we can pretty much arrive at a sound conclusion, or at least we can work out something that those with whom we disagree can agree with. In our text, the chapter on Rogerian argument especially emphasizes this point, and we want to say again that we think there is a good deal to it.

And yet honesty compels us to say that our lives—in and out of the classroom—have brought us also to another view, a view that is stated eloquently by Isaiah Berlin in a small collection of essays called *The Crooked Timber of Humanity* (1991). In one essay, "The Pursuit of the Ideal," he mentions that Tolstoy and many of his contemporaries held

> the belief that solutions to the central problems existed, that one could discover them, and, with sufficient selfless effort, realize them on earth. They all believed that the essence of human beings was to be able to choose how to live: societies could be transformed in the light of true ideals believed in with enough fervour and dedication. (3–4)

Berlin goes on, later in the essay, to say that "There are many different ends that men may seek and still be fully rational," and here we must quote him at some length:

> What is clear is that values can clash—that is why civilisations are incompatible. They can be incompatible between cultures, or groups in the same culture, or between you and me. You believe in always telling the truth, no matter what; I do not because I believe that it can sometimes be too painful and too destructive. We can discuss each other's point of view, we can try to reach common ground, but in the end what you pursue may not be reconcilable

with the ends to which I find that I have dedicated my life. Values may easily clash within the breast of a single individual; and it does not follow that, if they do, some must be true and others false. Justice, rigorous justice, is for some people an absolute value, but it is not compatible with what may be no less ultimate values for them—mercy, compassion—as arises in concrete cases. (12)

These words seem wise to us, and indeed they have helped us to get through some faculty meetings in which we briefly thought of murdering our colleagues. They have also helped us to get through some class hours in which we briefly thought of taking up some other line of work. The truth is, on certain polarizing issues there is no middle way: Today, abortion and capital punishment are prime examples. Yes, negotiation takes place—for instance, one can agree that teenagers may not be executed—but the fact is, capital punishment either is lawful or not. Similarly, one can negotiate about whether abortion may or may not be performed in the case of incest and rape, but the issue remains: A fetus either may be aborted or not.

This sort of thinking has emboldened us to include in *Current Issues* not only case-books, where multiple views are heard, but also a few debates, where we get pairs of strongly opposed voices. In our headnote to these debates, we call attention to the limits of binary thinking, and we caution students that some *either/or* arguments may be reductive, but again, we think it is healthy to recognize that on some issues, persons of intelligence and good faith may ultimately disagree.

Finally, we want to end this self-indulgent meditation by quoting a passage from Kenneth Burke's *The Philosophy of Literary Form* (1941), a passage that, like the passages from Burke and Mill, we also quote in our text because we want students to know them.

> Imagine that you enter a parlor. You come late. When you arrive, others have long preceded you, and they are engaged in a heated discussion, a discussion too heated for them to pause and tell you exactly what it is about. In fact, the discussion had already begun long before any of them got there, so that no one present is qualified to retrace for you all the steps that had gone before. You listen for a while, until you decide that you have caught the tenor of the argument; then you put in your oar. Someone answers; you answer him; another comes to your defense; another aligns himself against you, to either the embarrassment or grati-fication of your opponent, depending upon the quality of your ally's assistance. However, the discussion is interminable. The hour grows late, you must depart. And you do depart, with the discussion still vigorously in progress. (110–11)

Most of the essays in Part Four (five debates) are fairly short. As we suggested earlier, you may want to use one or more of these pairs when assigning the first five chapters, in discussions of such matters as assumptions, evidence, and tone.

Because these topics have inspired much writing in the last few years, they can be used to introduce students to new ways of finding sources. Each pair of debates can, however, be taken by itself. By the time a student has read both sides of one debate, he or she is in a pretty good position to write an essay on the issue or to analyze one of the arguments.

14
Student Loans: Should Some Indebtedness Be Forgiven? (p. 465)

First, a bit of background gathered from an article in the *New York Times*, September 9, 2012.

At the time of the article,

- About 5.9 million people had fallen at least twelve months behind in making payments.
- One in six borrowers was in default.
- Defaulted loans added up to about $76 billion.
- In 2011, the Department of Education paid $1.4 billion to private collection agencies to find defaulters.
- In 1211, the average default was $17,005.
- Borrowers who attended profit-making colleges—about 11 percent of all students—accounted for nearly half of the defaults. (A loan is declared in default when it is delinquent for 360 days.)
- Although defaulters often try to avoid detection, for instance by changing their telephone number, almost all defaulters are located.
- Only about 1 percent of the debtors are written off, usually because of death or disability.

Barbara Smaller (cartoon)

I'm looking for a career (p. 132)

It is a commonplace today that the job one prepares for will have changed by the time one begins the job. In the last decade even the profession of teaching has changed vastly because of new technology—no laughing matter for oldsters who have difficulty coping even with e-mail and attachments. In fact, one of today's standard arguments on behalf of a more-or-less traditional liberal arts education is that it teaches the student how to *think*, which in a swiftly changing world is more important than teaching a particular subject matter or a particular skill. The idea in this argument (we don't say it is true; we just say it is common) is that subject matter changes, and skills (e.g., how to use a slide rule) become obsolete, but habits of critical thinking, accompanied by a mind well-stocked with the achievements of the past, provide tools for adapting to changing conditions.

Robert Applebaum

Debate on Student Loan Debt Doesn't Go Far Enough (p. 465)

Applebaum's essay certainly is "bold," to use a word that he himself uses in his first paragraph.

It may be a good idea to ask students to search out his assumptions. As we see it, among his assumptions are these:

- Colleges, seeing "free money" (i.e., dollars paid in tuition by poor students who put themselves into debt), outrageously started to overpay administrators, and to build handsome but unnecessary facilities.

- Starting salaries are nowhere near enough to enable students to repay the loans, so students now learn that they bought a product (an education that was supposed to get them a job with a decent salary) at a ridiculously inflated price.

- Forgiveness of debt thus is not a handout but is closer to a refund.

- Students will spend the forgiven debt, thus boosting the economy.

Applebaum explicitly says (para. 3), "The Student Loan Forgiveness Act of 2012 is not a free ride, nor is it a bailout." In his view, he and his fellow borrowers were defrauded. Education "is a public good" (para. 4), and therefore "Education should be a right" (para. 5). It follows, then (at least for Applebaum), that the members of his generation should not be shackled with debt (in para. 6 he speaks of "indentured servitude") in order to get the education that society needs.

Well, one certainly knows where Applebaum stands. In our view, the next essay, by Justin Wolfers, demolishes Applebaum's economic argument, *but* we do think that Applebaum's fourth paragraph makes good sense. We here quote most of the paragraph:

> Every other country in the industrialized world has figured out how to pay for higher education for its citizens, but here in America, we continue to treat education as a commodity that benefits only the individual obtaining the education, rather than what it truly is: a public good and an investment in our collective future as a country.

Discuss. (We should add that although in this passage he speaks of education as a public good, and as an investment in the future of the nation, it seems to us that elsewhere in the essay he speaks about a college education as something that is valuable only because of the dollars that it apparently entitles the degree holder to earn.)

Justin Wolfers

Forgive Student Loans? Worst Idea Ever (p. 469)

Wolfers, an economist, looks at Applebaum's essay only as an economist. That is, he is concerned with Applebaum's argument that the economy will thrive if the government forgives each indebted student $50,000. Wolfers does not address the issue of whether or not higher education is (as Applebaum claims) a "right."

We think his response sounds pretty convincing, though we also think that Applebaum raises an issue in his fourth paragraph (we quote most of the paragraph in this manual, in our brief comment on Applebaum's essay) that must be seriously considered. In short, it is our guess that Wolfers is right in saying (in his final sentence) that no economist will agree with Applebaum, but we continue to think that Applebaum's essay raises—admittedly, in an almost incidental way—a significant issue concerning the role of education in a democracy, an issue that goes beyond the question of loan forgiveness.

15
Are Integrated Devices Safer Than Handheld Devices While Driving? (p. 471)

Mitch Bainwol

Pro (p. 471)

Our first question in the text invites students to think about Bainwol's assumptions. His underlying assumption, we think, is that people will insist on using phones in cars, though he does not put it this way. Rather than saying that drivers will talk on phones, he says that "consumers are going to communicate" (para. 6) and that "drivers are going to insist on staying connected behind the wheel" (para. 10). That is, he uses language with positive connotations ("communicate," "insist on staying connected") to describe what an opponent might call yakking or, at best, conversing.

A few other obvious points: In his first paragraph Bainwol admits there is a problem, "distracted driving"—but in this paragraph he also shrewdly sets up boundaries: The question, he says, is "how . . . to ameliorate it in the real world where drivers demand connectivity." That is, by speaking of the real world, and by claiming that drivers "demand connectivity," he in effect tries at the very outset to rule out of bounds (or at least to label as unrealistic) any counterview that in effect says that drivers should be prohibited from using phones while driving. Similarly, his assertion in his second paragraph that "technology has transformed our society forever" implies that we *must* live with the new technology.

In short, before he gets around to offering *evidence*, he has made assertions that—if a reader accepts them—pretty much make it unnecessary for Bainwol to offer any evidence, or to face and rebut counterviews. Thus, in Bainwol's view, to demand that drivers *not* use phones (again, in his words, give up "connectivity" and cease to "communicate") is to "put our heads in the sand and demand a behavioral shift," that is, to act in an utterly foolish manner. (Our second question in the text alludes to Bainwol's allusion [para. 4] to the popular belief that an ostrich, when pursued, buries its head in the sand and thus, because it cannot see its enemy, thinks that it cannot be seen. Not all students are familiar with this image that connotes the folly of thinking that a problem will go away if we pretend it doesn't exist.)

Bainwol's argument, then, is that attempts to banish communication are unrealistic, and fortunately technology has produced "integrated systems" that operate as a "safety filter," a filter that "mitigates accident risk and saves lives" (para. 5). He ends his essay by reaffirming his assumption that drivers insist on "staying connected behind the wheel," and that the real issue, then, is to "construct policy" that requires drivers to use the technology. Just that. (To put one's trust in a policy of banning the use of phones while driving is, he has explained, to behave like an ostrich.)

While we are talking about persons who defend the use of phones in automobiles, we may as well list the commonest arguments that we have heard, even though Bainwol doesn't offer them:

1. Phones are valuable in times of emergencies (e.g., drivers can call to report accidents they see on the road, or a vehicle that is driving erratically).

2. Distractions other than phones (e.g., conversing with a passenger, eating, lighting a cigarette, adjusting a mirror) probably cause a larger number of fatal accidents than talking on a telephone.

3. Police have more important jobs to do than looking for drivers who are using telephones.

4. If we really want to reduce accidents due to the use of phones, we should (a) educate drivers, and (b) urge them to purchase hands-free devices.

There are, of course, pretty good responses to all of these arguments, as you will hear in class if the issues come up.

OMG (Advertisement) (p. 473)

This advertisement, like most ads, uses words and imagery, but it probably is atypical in that the two media—at least at first glance—are equally impressive. Probably most ads use an image to hook the reader with a general message (e.g., a picture of an attractive family loading a car, in effect saying, "You can be like these happy folks"), and then some text for a more specific message to sell the particular brand of car. In the ad we reproduce, however, the text—"OMG" (text-talk for "oh my God")—and the image showing the spider-web pattern of the cracked and blood-stained glass both immediately seize our attention; the additional words, at the bottom, are important but decidedly ancillary.

We say "spider-web," but the image also evokes a target: In effect the image says, "If you text while driving, you are making yourself a deadly target." And the printed words, "Get the message," play on the business of sending messages, but this is no playful message, just as the large OMG is (*un*characteristically) *not* playful. The additional words ("Texting while driving is a deadly distraction") are almost unnecessary: The image and the texter's OMG do most of the work.

Incidentally, though initialism (that's what the specialists call such things as *OMG*, *LOL*, and *WTF*) is now especially associated with texting, it is really nothing new. Early examples: *AM, PM, FYI, PS, ROTC*.

Rob Reynolds

Con (p. 474)

We offer some responses to the questions that we raise in the text:

1. By using "so-called" (in "so-called naturalistic studies") Reynolds of course seeks to discredit the studies, implying that in fact they are not what their name claims them to be. The term "naturalistic studies" is new to us, but in the context, it pretty clearly means artificially constructed studies (i.e., carefully controlled studies) that apparently closely resemble real events.

2. Reynolds's use of "rigged with" (rather than "equipped with") is a nice example of the use of a negatively charged word in order to sway a reader.

3. By comparing those who defend the use of supposedly safer phones to the cigarette makers who defended filtered cigarettes, Reynolds of course seeks to discredit his opponents. Is the comparison fair? Or, to put it in the language associated with argument, is the analogy false? Our own view, as we state in our discussion of analogy, is that *all* analogies are "false," in that (to use the famous words of Bishop Joseph Butler) "Every thing is what it is, and not another thing." Take the famous adage, "Don't change horses in midstream," which usually in effect means (e.g., during a presidential election in a time of war), "Stay with the leader in this moment of crisis." Well, it is an effective line—it ordinarily makes good sense not to try to change one's mount while in the middle of a river—but, gee, choosing a different president to lead the government during a time of crisis is *not* really the

same as changing a mount in difficult circumstances. Again, "Every thing is what it is, and not another thing." Having said this, we want to add that we think the automakers who say, in effect, "Drivers will use these apps anyway; we just want to make it safer" are indeed pretty close to the cigarette makers who pushed filters. Still, there is a difference.

16
The Local Food Movement: Is It a Better Way to Eat? (p. 476)

First, a few words about "local" and "locavore." In speaking of food and farming, Congress has said that *local* (and *regional*) refer to food produced within four hundred miles of the place where it is sold, *or* food produced anywhere within the state in which it is sold. The word *locavore* (= consumer of local food) was coined in 2005.

Most farming is still a matter of planting in acres of dirt, but hydroponic greenhouses, where plants grow not in soil but in mineral-infused water, take up much less space, and they are proliferating. In these greenhouses, any crop can be produced all year round, whereas, for instance, a dirt farm in New England that produces strawberries can grow them for only about six weeks. Still, locally grown food is thought to constitute only about 1 percent of what we eat.

Second, a reminder: In Chapter 8, we print a relevant essay, James McWilliams's "The Locavore Myth."

Stephen Budiansky

Math Lessons for Locavores (p. 476)

Budiansky's opening paragraph seems prolocavore, but anyone with some experience reading arguments will sense that he is setting something up in order to knock it down. And in fact the title—"Math Lessons for Locavores"—implies that Budiansky will be putting down locavores.

We say "putting down," but perhaps those words are too strong. Certainly he lectures to locavores, but we find his tone acceptable—especially when compared with the fury of Kerry Trueman's response, which we reprint immediately after Budiansky's piece. But we will talk about Trueman's tone when we discuss her essay below. As for the present essay, we found it highly informative, and it struck us as forceful but within the bounds of courteous discourse. True, he uses such words as "self-indulgent," "do-gooders," "arbitrary," "thrown around," and "without any clear understanding," but we were not fully aware of this sort of language until we reread the piece. On first reading, we were fully taken by the details, and we pretty much looked *through* rather than *at* the language.

A word about the structure of the essay: Like many, many other writers, Budiansky ends by returning to a motif introduced in his first paragraph. We discuss this strategy in the parent text, when we talk about drafting an argument (p. 228).

Kerry Trueman

The Myth of the Rabid Locavore (p. 479)

From the very beginning—even from the title with "Myth" and "Rabid"—the essay is extremely belligerent: In the first paragraph we get "self-proclaimed," "stuffed together," "flimsy," "boilerplate," "patronizing"—all in one sentence. In the third paragraph things get even rougher, with some scatological humor:

Throw in a bunch of dubious and/or irrelevant statistics that appear to be truly locally sourced—i.e., pulled out of your own behind.

We do not doubt that Trueman makes some good points, but we think that if she toned it down a bit, she might be more convincing, more effective. For one thing, although she is annoyed by what she calls Budianski's patronizing title ("Math Lessons for Locavores"), she probably should have taken his title more seriously. He really is talking largely about math—especially the energy costs of transporting food. Thus, she scolds him for neglecting certain topics, such as "support for more ecological farming practices" and "more humane treatment of livestock." But a reader might reply, "Yes, the issues you name are certainly issues of immense importance, but the author of a very short essay called "Math Lessons for Locovores" ought not to be expected to include discussion of them.

What we are saying adds up to this: We think Trueman makes many good points, but by letting her righteous anger take over, she does a disservice to her argument and thus to her cause. We doubt that readers want to ally themselves with someone who says (para. 15), "Budiansky needs to be taken out to the foodshed and pummeled with his own lousy logic." In our text, when we discuss a writer's persona, we caution students against displays of ill temper that will alienate a reader. Trueman's essay may be a good illustration.

17
The Death Penalty: Is It Ever Justified? (p. 483)

Background

The continuing salience of the death penalty in our society (as well as the popularity of the topic with users of this book) encourages us to retain in this edition two essays (the debate between Edward Koch and David Bruck) and to use a third essay (by Sister Helen Prejean) later in the book, in Chapter 26, What Is the Ideal Society? Indeed, we reprint enough material to permit a modest research paper to be written on the strength of this chapter alone.

As a preface to these essays, here are some basic facts about the death penalty as of 2010, based on information provided by the federal Bureau of Justice Statistics, Amnesty International, the NAACP Legal Defense Fund, and the Death Penalty Information Center: About 3,400 people are currently under sentence of death in thirty-five states (fifteen states have no death penalty); all of these prisoners have been convicted of some form of criminal homicide. About 18,000 persons are homicide victims each year, about 14,000 persons are convicted of these crimes, and about 300 are sentenced to death. The overwhelming majority of persons on death row are male (nearly 99 percent); about half are white, and of the rest, some 1,500—or about 40 percent of the total—are African American. In 80 percent of the executions, the murder victim was white.

In the years since 1976, when the Supreme Court validated the constitutionality of the death penalty, 1,195 persons have been executed. The number of executions annually has ranged from zero in 1978 and 1980 to twenty-five in 1987 and sixty in 2005. The vast majority have occurred in the South; Texas has executed the most, and five states (Colorado, Idaho, New Mexico, Tennessee, and Wyoming) have executed only one; nine of the death-penalty jurisdictions have executed none. Nine states still use the electric chair, five use the gas chamber, three use hanging, one uses the firing squad, and thirty-six use lethal injection; seventeen allow the prisoner to choose between alternatives (for example, hanging or lethal injection).

In recent years, two-thirds of those on death row had a prior felony conviction; 8 percent had a prior conviction of criminal homicide.

The elapsed time between conviction and execution is considerable—ten to fifteen years is not uncommon—owing principally to the appeals taken in state and federal courts. Recently, roughly 40 percent of all death sentences have been reversed on appeal in federal courts. (It is not known how many were reinstituted by state courts after either retrial or resentencing.)

Our excerpts in this chapter do not attempt to present the "human" side of the death penalty—the experiences of the condemned waiting for execution on death row, the frustration inflicted on surviving relatives and friends of the deceased victim by the delays in carrying out the death sentence, the impossible demands made on attorneys on both sides to meet court-imposed deadlines. From among the many books devoted to these aspects of the whole controversy, two deserve mention. One is *Dead Man Walking* (1993), by a Roman Catholic nun, Sister Helen Prejean, focusing on her experiences in Louisiana. (The excerpt from this book that we reprint is focused on a different aspect of the whole subject.) The film of the same title, made from her book, available on videocassette and DVD, has proved to be a remarkable stimulus to classroom discussion. The other book is *Among the Lowest of the Dead* (1995), by a journalist, David Von Drehle, based on his extensive study of Florida's death-row prisoners. Neither book is devoted primarily to the argument pro or con, but each adds immeasurably to a better understanding of the impact of the current death-penalty system on individual lives.

Elsewhere in the world, according to Amnesty International, as of 2009, 95 countries have abolished the death penalty by law and another 122 by practice, including all of western Europe and all the eastern nations that were satellites of the former USSR (except Poland, which has had, since 1988, an unofficial moratorium on executions; Belarus still continues to use the death penalty).

Two essays we've previously included are George Ryan's "Speech Announcing Commutation of All Illinois Prisoners' Death Sentences" and Gary Wills' "The Dramaturgy of Death," both of which would supplement this debate nicely. Former governor Ryan's clemency statement is unique in offering a full-scale critique of capital punishment as it is actually practiced, in contrast to the more abstract discussions by other thinkers presented in this section. What the essay may lack in style, originality, and economy of language, it makes up with its earnest appeal to the sensibility and imagination of the audience.

Did Ryan's use of his clemency powers have much effect on the thinking and practices of other governors with large death-row populations? Not so far as we can tell, though the future may tell a different story. Could it be that Ryan has had few imitators because other governors have not had to face the awful truth that there are unquestionably innocent prisoners on their death rows?

The essay by Wills offers a novel approach to the discussion of the death penalty by taking a passage from Friedrich Nietzsche (written more than a century ago) in which he identifies and evaluates the purposes or functions of punishment generally. Wills then uses this larger framework to develop the special features of the death penalty. A total of fourteen such purposes or functions are identified, with the result that light is shed on the death penalty from each of these directions. Classroom discussion for at least two sessions could profitably be devoted to identifying how many of these topics that Nietzsche and Wills find relevant are found in the death-penalty practices currently used in America, along with an account of their relative importance.

Edward I. Koch

Death and Justice: How Capital Punishment Affirms Life (p. 483)

The controversy over the death penalty is a perennial focus of high school debate, and some students will have encountered the issue there. Extensive discussion of almost every claim advanced or contested by former New York City Mayor Edward I. Koch and by David Bruck (author of the following essay) can be found in the scholarly literature on the subject; for starters, look at *The Death Penalty in America: Current Controversies* (1997), edited by Hugo Bedau. An unusually extensive exchange in a modified debate format, between John Conrad and Ernest van den Haag, is found in their book, *The Death Penalty: A Debate* (1983).

Koch opens with several examples that hold our attention. They allow him to get the ironist's advantage by the end of his second paragraph ("their newfound reverence for life"), and they hint at his combative style, which helped make his autobiographical book, *Mayor* (1984), into a best seller.

Koch's essay is a bit unusual among those in the text because he adopts the strategy of advancing his side of the argument by succinctly stating and then criticizing the arguments of the other side. Because he is in control, of course, the other side has to be content with his selection and emphasis; by allowing the other side no more than a one-sentence statement per argument, he makes it look pretty unconvincing.

Koch's concluding paragraphs (15 and 16) are particularly strong because he manages to show his sensitivity to a major claim by the opposition ("the death of . . . even a convicted killer . . . diminishes us all"), even as he implies that the alternative he favors is nevertheless better than the one he opposes. The important details of his own position (question 5) he leaves unspecified.

David Bruck

The Death Penalty (p. 489)

David Bruck's style of argument can be usefully contrasted to Edward I. Koch's. Bruck begins not as Koch did with an example or two (Bruck offers his first example only at para. 4) but with a brief recap of Koch's central position — that morality requires society to execute the convicted murderer. Then, instead of a patient (tedious?) argument-by-argument examination of Koch's position, Bruck tries to make headway by rubbing our noses in some of the disturbing details about the plight of persons on death row that, he implies, cast a different light on the morality of executions.

He then directly challenges (paras. 7–8) one of Koch's principal factual contentions about the possibility of erroneous executions. While we're at it, we can correct Bruck when he writes that Hugo Bedau's research involved about 400 cases "in which the state eventually *admitted* error." The research showed that the state admitted error in 309 out of 350 cases — and also that no state has ever admitted executing an innocent person, although Bedau reports that his research shows twenty-three such erroneous executions since 1900. Subsequent to the Koch-Bruck debate, this research has been published in the book, *In Spite of Innocence* (1992), by Michael Radelet, Hugo Bedau, and Constance Putnam.

Worry over convicting the innocent in capital cases reached a new degree of intensity during 2000. In Illinois, prompted by the fact that in recent years as many death-row prisoners had been released because of their innocence as had been executed, Governor George Ryan declared a statewide moratorium on executions, to last until he could be assured that effective remedial procedures were in place. Thus Illinois became the first capital punishment jurisdiction to comply with the 1996 recommendation from the House of Delegates of the American Bar Association, urging a nationwide moratorium on the death penalty until procedures were introduced to ensure fairness, due process, and competent counsel for capital defendants. Much of the background to Ryan's decision is discussed in the recent book *Actual Innocence* (2000) by Jim Dwyer, Peter Neufeld, and Barry Scheck. They relate the stories of recent cases (many, but not all, of them involving the use of DNA evidence to exonerate the innocent) that show just how easy it is for the innocent to be convicted and sentenced to death.

In the Koch-Bruck debate, the mayor had the last word, although we didn't reprint it in the text. His objections to Bruck's rebuttal may be found in *The New Republic* (May 20, 1985, p. 21). The main assertion in Koch's response is that "a truly civilized society need not shrink from imposing capital punishment as long as its procedures for determining guilt and passing sentence are constitutional and just." The reader of Koch's original article may well wonder where in it he succeeded in showing that these "procedures" in our society, as actually administered, are "just."

A word about question 4, on the polygraph or "lie detector." The so-called lie detector does not, of course, detect lies. It records physiological phenomena such as abnormal heart beat that are commonly associated with lying. Opponents say it is based on the premise that there is a "Pinocchio effect," a bodily response unique to lying. Opponents of the polygraph argue that the effects recorded, such as an increased heart rate or blood pressure, can have other causes. That is, these changes may reflect personal anxieties apart from lying, and, on the other hand, the symptoms may be suppressed by persons who in fact are lying. Wu-Tai Chin, the CIA employee who spied for China for thirty years, "passed" polygraph tests many times. The American Psychological Association, after a two-year study, concluded flatly that polygraph tests are "unsatisfactory." It is also noteworthy that findings from polygraphs are not admitted as evidence in federal courts.

18
Genetic Modification of Human Beings: Is It Acceptable? (p. 495)

Ronald M. Green

Building Baby from the Genes Up (p. 495)

The essential body of the argument raised in Green's essay appears in his discussion of the "four major concerns" raised by genetic engineering. He presents them in the following order (Does he regard this order as a reflection of their relative importance?): (1) adverse effects on parenting, (2) a diminution in our freedom of action, (3) aggravating undesirable social class conflicts, and (4) playing God. It is not much of a surprise when we learn that he is not persuaded by any of these arguments, much less all. Neither are we. Our take on this quartet of reasons places the most popular argument, (4), at the bottom of the list. As for the other three, our hunch is that it's a dead heat.

Green asks (Is it a rhetorical question?), "Why should a child struggle with reading difficulties when we could alter the genes responsible for the problem?" (para. 4). Several reasons might lead a thoughtful critic to conclude that we cannot afford such genetic engineering. One of these reasons might be that there is the risk of terrible side effects in erasing the genes relevant to reading difficulties. Even if there were few or no risks of such side effects, there might be a very high economic cost in implementing such genetic interventions. Yet another reason might be the unreliability of the diagnosis. The sum of these costs might be properly regarded as outweighing the benefits. Or so those who oppose such biochemical interventions might argue. Green does not explore this territory as deeply as one might wish.

He loads the dice (in whose favor?) when (in para. 5) he invokes the 1997 science fiction film *Gattaca*. In the world of Gattaca, "its eugenic obsessions have all but extinguished human love and compassion." Since we are dealing entirely with a fictitious society (with unmistakable overtones of Aldous Huxley's *Brave New World* [1932]), why not depict one in which the eugenic designers have figured out ways to increase human love and compassion, a cheerful disposition, happiness, and to foster traits such as honesty, altruism, pacific temperament, and other virtues? Green comes close to this idea in his closing paragraph.

Richard Hayes

Genetically Modified Humans? No Thanks (p. 499)

Hayes offers the reader a full-scale assault on Ronald Green's essay. His sole concession to those who side with Green is the use of genetic engineering to save lives and cure illnesses. He explicitly rejects genetic modifications designed to yield "heritable genetic enhancement" (paras. 7 and 8). He criticizes Green for failing to distinguish these two different uses of genetic modification and he enlists "public opinion" and the laws of "nearly 40 countries" that agree with him.

Hayes gives a beautiful example of invoking the slippery slope argument, worth quoting in full: "Once we begin genetically modifying our children, where do we stop?" (para. 3). Hayes seems not to notice that this objection will arise against even the limited use of the genetic modifications he would allow. Once the genie is out of the bottle—well, you can write the script for the rest of the parade of horrors that Hayes offers us. Hayes also thinks that "Green most fervently wants us to embrace . . . heritable genetic enhancement" (para. 7). This makes Green look like a rabid fanatic, not at all consistent with the style in which he presents himself to the reader. And irresponsible as well, when he says that "Green blithely announces his confidence" (para. 9). We think that a fairer assessment of Green's essay would reveal a cautious exploration of a highly controversial social policy on which we are a long way from having said the last word on either side of the debate.

Part Five

CURRENT ISSUES: CASEBOOKS

19
A College Education: What Is Its Purpose? (p. 505)

Andrew Delbanco

3 Reasons College Still Matters (p. 505)

We begin indirectly, by offering at the outset not a discussion of Delbanco but a famous quotation by William Cory (1823–1892), a schoolmaster at Eton. And, indeed, when he talks about going to a "school," he means a school, not a college or a university. But we think his words apply very well to a college—most obviously to a liberal arts college but, we will briefly argue, also to colleges that emphasize vocational training. Here is Cory's quotation, taken from a letter he wrote.:

> At school you are engaged not so much in acquiring knowledge as in making mental efforts under criticism. A certain amount of knowledge you can indeed with average faculties acquire so as to retain; nor need you regret the hours you spent on much that is forgotten, for the shadow of lost knowledge at least protects you from many illusions. But you go to a great school not so much for knowledge as for arts and habits; for the habit of attention, for the art of expression, for the art of assuming at a moment's notice a new intellectual position, for the art of entering quickly into another person's thoughts, for the habit of submitting to censure and refutation, for the art of indicating assent or dissent in graduated terms, for the habit of regarding minute points of accuracy, for the art of working out what is possible in a given time, for taste, for discrimination, for mental courage, and for mental soberness. Above all, you go to a great school for self-knowledge.

These words pretty much embody our idea of a liberal education—especially, if we had to choose just a phrase or so, the passage about acquiring the habit of "indicating assent or dissent in graduated terms." Cory is speaking about what today is called "critical thinking," a topic we discuss at length in our first three chapters. It is our belief that most liberal arts courses—*and especially introductory courses in composition or argument or rhetoric*—inevitably are largely devoted to this sort of thinking. We grant, however, that some courses are not, for instance, introductory courses in which a student learns a foreign language—although even in the earliest stages of learning a foreign language one begins to see things from an unaccustomed point of view!

What about courses that are designed to prepare a student for a particular career, let's say a course in accounting for a business major or a course in psychology for a nursing major? It is our strong impression that almost all such courses *do* require students to enter "into another person's thoughts," *do* develop "the habit of regarding minute points of accuracy," *do* help a student to master "the art of working out what is possible in a given time," and they *do* help to develop "taste, . . . discrimination, . . . mental courage, and . . . mental soberness." Admittedly, such courses usually do not introduce a student to unfamiliar Great Ideas—they do not immediately present students with challenging new conceptions—but we believe that almost all college courses (in two-year colleges as well as four-year colleges), sometimes almost in spite of themselves, help students to achieve "self-knowledge."

End of sermon on the value of college courses, including those offered by programs with a decided vocational slant.

Delbanco offers three reasons on behalf of acquiring a liberal education: (1) It enables people to live better lives; (2) a democracy requires educated citizens; and (3) a liberal education helps a person to "enjoy life" (para. 16). The last might seem frivolous, but he puts it in the culminating or climactic position. Our seventh question in the text asks students to comment on Delbanco's sequence. We ourselves are entirely satisfied with his arrangement, but of course other arrangement might be equally satisfactory. He might have led off with this relatively personal angle and then moved to the grander social aspects. Indeed, Delbanco risked—with the arrangement that he settled on—descending with a bump, trivializing the issue, but (again) we find his arrangement satisfactory. In our view, this relatively modest reason (allegedly suggested to him by an alumnus) allows him to end in a down-to-earth manner.

We are *not* saying that the sequence of the three points really doesn't matter; rather, we are saying that it *does* matter, and that a different sequence would produce a somewhat different essay. Delbanco is writing for the general public—or, rather, that part of the general public that reads articles and books about the value of a college education. If he had been writing in a journal that is read chiefly by college administrators, we think he might have put this business about pleasure first and then gone on to discuss the grander issues. But given his audience, he chose to end with a down-to-earth reason. Seems good to us.

Patrick Allitt

Should Undergraduates Specialize? (p. 510)

By all means, permit young would-be physicists to pursue physics from the get-go—(our answer to question 2); they ought to be "free" to do so. But let us teachers and course advisers also try to persuade them to broaden their collegiate studies. They might not have another chance until they retire and can take a postgraduate extension course in the Great Books of Western Civilization. A freshman humanities course for all students, whatever their major fields, can go a long way toward providing a minimal exposure to some area of history, literature, philosophy, and fine arts—the Renaissance and Reformation, say— without overburdening the science students' program of studies.

Some students, especially those born abroad or born of parents who were educated abroad, may be familiar with a system of higher education that differs from American higher education. If you have any such students, you may want to ask them to comment on the system and to indicate what they think are its strengths and weaknesses.

A few other points, chiefly about Patrick Allitt's ways of arguing: We think it is worth mentioning that the essay is somewhat unusual in its emphasis on the first person. Allitt draws on his own experience as a student, and also on his experience as the father of a woman who is now in college. In short, we tell students, writers of arguments often cite authorities, and there are some instances in which the writers themselves are authorities. If a student is writing about an issue in which he or she has been significantly involved, there is no reason to hesitate to draw on this firsthand experience.

A second point concerning Allitt's argument is this: The argument is a comparison, and inexperienced writers can learn from Allitt some ways of organizing a comparison. Notice that in his first paragraph he introduces the basic issue—his own education versus his daughter's—and in his second paragraph he indicates that "these two college adventures differ sharply." Readers know exactly what to expect. The next four paragraphs are devoted to talking about his own education, and then, in the seventh paragraph, we get a clear transition: "Frances, by contrast, is entering a decentralized system." And of course we then get several paragraphs devoted to the American system. There is none of that dizzying back-and-forth ping-pong structure of alternating paragraphs with "A is this, B is that," "Thus A, while B," "Again A, whereas B. . . ." We don't say that one should never alternate paragraphs when writing a comparison, but many students have been told in high school that a proper comparison keeps going back and forth. Nonsense. There is nothing wrong with indicating the nature of the comparison at the outset, then setting forth one half, and then setting forth the other half. Of course in setting forth the second half, one must be careful to establish connections with the first half, usually by very briefly reminding the reader of this or that feature. The comparisons that break apart are those that set forth a block and then set forth a second block *and do not connect the second with the first*. Allitt's essay clearly is not guilty of this error.

Finally, we note—and this point is obvious—Allitt ends by focusing on American education. His final paragraph is not "Thus we see that in England A, but in America Y." Rather—because his real point is American education—he devotes all of the final paragraph to American education.

Carlo Rotella

No, It Doesn't Matter What You Majored In (p. 516)

Rotella's eighth (i.e., his-next-to-last) paragraph ends by saying that a college graduate ought to be able to "deliver a sustained reasoned argument. . . . It's a craft, like cabinet making." Obviously there are two points here, one about the college graduate as someone who can reason, and a second about reasoning as a craft, an acquired skill. We are inclined to agree with both points: The author/editors of a textbook on critical thinking (Rotella's "reasoned argument") of course believe that this subject can be taught, which is to say that students can *learn* to "deliver a sustained reasoned argument," and they believe students can learn how to do this because reasoning is (or, better, it *largely* is) a "craft," that is, something with basic principles that reasonably intelligent people can master.

Now, of course there is more to a liberal education than the ability to reason. Briefly, we subscribe also to a statement from Allan Bloom's *The Closing of the American Mind*:

> The liberally educated person is one who is able to resist the easy and preferred answers, not because he is obstinate but because he knows others worthy of consideration.

But this is *not* to say (in our view) that the only "liberal" courses are those evidently devoted to Big Ideas, World Classics, and so on. An introductory course in (say) anthropology might well bring the student into contact with someone from a culture notably different from his or her own, a culture that offers unfamiliar views: A Caucasian student might find herself interviewing a Chinese immigrant, or even a first-generation American Chinese, and might thus come into contact with unfamiliar ideas "worthy of consideration." Indeed the cultures need not be so evidently different: Encountering someone whose religious beliefs are different, or whose economic status is different, can have profound educational effects.

And—here we add a self-congratulatory note—we think that the essays in our text go a long way toward introducing students to unfamiliar ideas that are (in Bloom's words) "worthy of consideration." Students (including those enrolled in programs that essentially are designed to prepare them for careers in business or nursing or police work or engineering or whatever) who are familiar with these readings are learning to think about ideas that are worthy of consideration.

Alina Tugend

Vocation or Exploration: Pondering the Purpose of College (p. 518)

Perhaps foolishly (though of course we don't think so), we have touched on *vocational* education in our comments on the essays by Delbanco and Rotella, so we urge you to glance at those discussions (above) in this manual. The gist of our view is that many courses usually regarded as vocational can in fact contribute to a liberal education.

Mark Edmundson

Education's Hungry Hearts (p. 521)

We think this essay presents no difficulties even to inexperienced readers, and here we will confine ourselves to offering our responses to some of the questions we raise in the text.

1. Our first question concerns the effectiveness of the title and the opening paragraph. If the term "Hungry Hearts" is known to the reader, from Bruce Springsteen's song, it will certainly arouse attention (which of course is what the *exordium* of a speech is supposed to do), but even if it is not known, the phrase itself stirs some interest: The reader wants to know, "Well, who are these 'hungry hearts,' and exactly what about them?" The first paragraph identifies the source of the phrase—and presumably convinces the reader to stay with the essay, since the reader knows who Springsteen is and now wants to know how this term and this popular figure are going to to fit into an essay that appeared in the *New York Times*.

   The first paragraph is engagingly colloquial, with its "Really?" and its "Is that so?" and when he goes on at the end of the first paragraph to say, "At the risk of offending the Boss, I want to register some doubts," presumably the reader is hooked, that is, will stay with the piece in order to learn what the doubts are.

   The second paragraph, still part of the opening—that is, the part of the essay in which the writer (we might almost say the speaker or even the rhetorician) gets the hearers' attention, establishes his or her own bona fides, and sets out the issue—is highly personal. We learn that Edmundson has taught for thirty-five years and has had some four thousand students, so we are presumably willing to grant that he is highly experienced, and he ought to have something interesting to say about students and about education. Of course by the time readers finish the essay they may conclude that they were mistaken in this assumption—that despite the author's experience, he has nothing to say—but, again, we think that a reader on first encountering this paragraph is inclined to assume that the essayist is worth listening to. In rhetorical terms, Edmundson here is concerned with *ethos*, that is, with presenting himself as someone of goodwill.

   And, to put it bluntly, his argument rests almost entirely on this presentation of himself as someone who ought to be listened to on this topic. He offers nothing in the way of statistics, nothing in the way of deductive logic, nothing in the way of authorities. Yes, he does mention such names as Freud, Kafka, Blake, Nietzsche, and Lionel Trilling, but not as authorities on what college has to offer, or what kinds of students are the best students. On these issues, we have to trust Edmundson, whose evidence is the four thousand students who have passed his desk—he offers some generalizations about good and bad students—and some other persons whom he has encountered, for instance, his friend Paul Rizzo, a person utterly unknown to the reader. If we are impressed by this sort of inductive evidence, it is because Edmundson has presented himself as the sort of guy that readers like and can identify themselves with, someone who is not whining, someone who does not have a chip on his shoulder, someone who is not essentially advancing his own agenda but, rather, someone who is concerned with the general welfare. Again (and in short), a matter of persuasion by *ethos*.

2. Our second question following the essay is about Edmundson's concluding paragraph—the paragraph in which he tells us about Paul Rizzo's current life. As we have just said, this is hardly proof if one is thinking of proof as logical argument, but we think the paragraph is at least moderately effective as a piece of persuasive writing. A reader sort of *likes* this Rizzo guy and is impressed with him, even though the reader knows almost nothing about him.

3. Where, if anywhere, does Edmundson explicitly state his thesis? The thesis is implied in paragraphs 4 and 5 and is stated explicitly in his sixth paragraph, just before the middle of this short essay. In a long essay, a reader certainly wants the thesis to be stated earlier than just before the middle, but in an essay of the length of Edmundson's, we think the position is satisfactory; that is the reader learns it within a minute.

4. As we have been saying, Edmundson offers very little in the way of *reasons*—and that is partly why we offer it early in the book. He doesn't give statistics, he doesn't cite relevant authorities, he doesn't offer syllogisms. He offers himself, *ethos*. (We don't use this word until our third chapter, but there is no harm—indeed, there can be much merit—in an instructor introducing it earlier.)

Marty Nemko

America's Most Overrated Product: The Bachelor's Degree (p. 523)

We have not taught this essay, but we imagine that it will produce much discussion in classrooms, both in two-year and in four-year institutions.

Nemko describes himself as a "career counselor," and it may well be that, face-to-face with a given individual, he can give sound advice that will save the person tens of thousands of dollars and will also enable the advisee to have a happy career. Certainly the scenario he establishes in his first paragraph (a student who did poorly in high school tells Nemko that he or she has been attending college for five years, is $80,000 in debt, and still has 45 credits to go) is distressing, which means that it is an effective piece of writing. Nemko's second paragraph is also effective: He offers "the killer statistic" that 40 percent of the people who graduated in the bottom 40 percent of their classes, and whose first institutions are four-year colleges, will not have earned a diploma eight and a half years later. And he follows this assertion with an assertion that pretty clearly implies that many four-year colleges are engaged in a con game: "Yet four-year colleges admit and take money from hundreds of thousands of such students each year!"

So here is our problem with the essay: On the one hand, Nemko's title is catchy and probably has a good deal of truth to it; he seems to know what he is talking about (he cites statistics), and his sympathy is with the underdog, but the suggestion that colleges are engaged in a swindle makes us a bit uneasy, even a bit suspicious. Yes, no doubt admissions officers are aware that there are desks and beds to be filled—in other words, that a certain number of tuition-paying students is needed to keep the place going—but the cynicism implied in "take money from hundreds of thousands of students" unnerves us. Perhaps we are unnerved because we fear the assertion may be true, but we think our uneasiness proceeds from a sense that Nemko thinks of college only in terms of dollars and cents and the higher incomes that college graduates earn. By the way, Nemko's assertion that college graduates of course earn more because "they're bright, more motivated, and have better family connections" (para. 5) seems to us to be only partly true: They do have better family connections, and they probaby are more motivated so far as making money goes, but we are not sure that they are brighter. We have met plenty of very bright carpenters, plumbers, electricians, beauticians, musicians—and indeed gardeners and butchers and farmers. Academic success probably ought not to be equated with brightness. Or, put it this way: People can be smart in different ways. But yes, a college degree probably does tell an employer that the job candidate is fairly intelligent, fairly diligent, fairly socialized. The employer may then believe, "This is the person for me. As for specialized skills needed for this particular job, well, X can learn them here; what I want is someone who is fairly intelligent, fairly diligent, fairly socialized, and the bachelor's degree probably is a sign of these qualities."

In his eighth paragraph Nemko casts a cold eye on the colleges' assertion that "A college education is more about enlightenment than employment," and he brings up the issue of large lecture classes, implying that students are getting short-changed: The small classes are taught mostly (he says) by graduate students. We think there is much to be said for senior professors—or at least those of them who are good with small groups—teaching some small classes, but we also believe that a large lecture course can be highly effective.

We have already mentioned that Nemko uses statistics. In his second paragraph, for instance, he speaks of "a study cited by Clifford Adelman," and in his ninth paragraph he speaks of "the latest annual national survey of freshmen conducted by the Higher Education Research Institute," but he never gets around to giving exact titles and specific page references, and we have the feeling (admittedly merely a feeling) that the studies may be more nuanced than Nemko suggests. For instance, in his ninth paragraph Nemko mentions a study that reports that 44.6 percent of the freshmen surveyed "said they were not satisfied with the quality of instruction they received." But exactly what was the context, what was the exact queston the students were asked? For instance, if the students were indeed talking about their courses as a whole—in other words, their academic experience in college thus far (as we think Nemko implies)—the figure is indeed alarming. But what if the response was given to a question such as "Are you satisfied with the instruction in all of the courses that you have taken?" Or "Were you dissatisfied with the instruction in any course?" Surely, it will not be surprising or distressing to learn that a student taking four courses, some of which are required rather than elected, is unhappy with one or even two. Furthermore, anyone who has served on a tenure committee and has read dozens or even hundreds of students' evaluations of a candidate for tenure knows that the range of responses may be wide: 10 percent of the students say a given course is the best they have had, 80 percent say the course is pretty good, and the remaining 10 percent say they got little or maybe nothing from the course.

What about Nemko's bulleted proposals, for example, that colleges post on their Web sites the results of a "value added" test? Well, we are all in favor of transparency, and it would indeed be interesting to see the statistics that he calls for, though it is hard to imagine that colleges would or could comply. To take a single instance: How likely is it that colleges can gather the "salary data" of graduates (sixth bullet)?

Our final comment: We are inclined to agree with Nemko's last paragraph (it begins, "College is a wise choice for far fewer people than are currently encouraged to consider it"), but we think that his somewhat belligerent tone and his failure to give exact citations for his sources weaken his essay.

Charles Murray

Should the Obama Generation Drop Out? (p. 528)

We are not quite sure what to make of this essay. We imagine that most people—instructors as well as undergraduates—will agree with the last sentence in Murray's opening paragraph, "It's what you can do that should count when you apply for a job, not where you learned to do it." But we don't see how he gets from this position to one of his basic assumptions, stated in his fourth paragraph:

> For most of the nation's youths, making the bachelor's degree a job qualification means demanding a credential that is beyond their reach. It is a truth that politicians and educators cannot bring themselves to say out loud: A large majority of young people do not have the intellectual ability to do genuine college-level work.

Curiously, in his next few paragraphs Murray offers as proof the readers' inability today to succeed in a subject other than their chosen major:

> You think I'm too pessimistic? Too elitist? Readers who graduated with honors in English literature or Renaissance history should ask themselves if they could have gotten a B.S. in physics, no matter how hard they tried. (I wouldn't have survived freshman year.) Except for the freakishly gifted, all of us are too dumb to get through college in many majors.

74

This may well be true—but, at least as we see it, these assertions argue against Murray's basic point that "a large majority of young people do not have the intellectual ability to do genuine college-level work." He seems to be saying that college graduates—such as his readers and Murray himself—could not graduate if they had been forced to major in certain fields, and this is somehow taken to be proof that most of today's youngsters are unfit for college. Unless he is saying—and we do not think this is his point—that his own inability to handle physics shows that he himself does not have "the intellectual ability to do genuine college-level work," the evidence he offers indicates that indeed a person can be weak in one area or another, and yet still do creditable work in several other areas. That is, the evidence Murray offers—the reader's inability to do good work in all academic areas—undercuts his own position, since he assumes that his reader is a college graduate.

Probably most colleges and universities recognize that students have varying competencies, and they offer a variety of courses suited to these differences. For instance, there may be an introductory physics course that is designed for would-be physicists, and quite another physics course—still respectable—designed for the nonspecialist. Or take composition courses: A college may (1) exempt some students from the basic course, and (2) require some other students to take a one-term course, and (3) require yet other students to take a two-term course.

As we understand it, Murray is talking about two topics which are barely related: One topic is

Unfortunately, a College Education Is Now Regarded as a Pre-Requisite for Most Jobs, Even for Jobs That Should Not Require It.

and a second topic is

Most Young People Are Not Fit to Go to College.

Our own view is that he is right about the first of these topics and wrong about the second. But our view doesn't matter: What matters is Murray's essay, which is a good example of an essay that lacks focus.

Let's talk only about his proposal that potential employers stop asking for a college degree. He suggests two alternatives: "certification tests" (paras.1–12) and "samples" (or "examples") of the candidate's work. Certainly, samples of work ought to do the trick in some areas (let's say, jewelry making, or—Murray's own example—computer programming), but "certification tests" seem to us to be a bad idea. Is Murray talking about a sort of SAT for this job and that job? Who would make the tests for, say, the job of an editorial assistant at a textbook publisher, a car salesman, or a receptionist at a health center? And who would score them? And how many people would agree that indeed the tests test what they are supposed to test?

Briefly, then, we agree with Murray's proposed battle cry, "It's what you can do that should count when you apply for a job, not where you learned to do it," and we strongly approve of his decision to use this very line again as the last line of his essay. (Here he is following the sound rhetorical strategy of returning, in the final paragraph, to a topic introduced in the opening, a strategy that we suggest in our book, where we talk about concluding paragraphs.) We also agree that the widespread requirement of a degree—even for jobs that do not require anything learned at college—is deplorable. Young persons who want to be carpenters or chefs or gardeners or fishermen or actors or writers, and whose experiences in high school have convinced them that they do not wish to undergo further academic training, should be encouraged to engage in their chosen fields. But of course persons with these same ambitions, if they wish to go first to college, should be encouraged to do so, which means, among other things, that somehow college should be made financially possible for them. They probably will, we think, live better lives as carpenters, chefs, gardeners, fishermen, actors, and writers than if they had not gone to college. But we digress: We will again say (1) we are skeptical of some of Murray's proposed solutions, and (2) we very much doubt his assumption that "A large majority of young people do not have the intellectual ability to do genuine college-level work" (para. 4).

Louis Menand

Re-imagining Liberal Education (p. 534)

Vocationalism (question 3) is a neologism derived from vocation, which in turn comes from the Latin for "calling," now a rather dated expression. Lawyers were once said to be called to the bar; doctors, and especially clerics, were said to have a calling—or to lack one, if they were so unfortunate. Who is to do the calling and how one is to decide whether he or she has been called to medicine, or to teaching, or to some other career or profession is not obvious. In our time, few, if any, teachers would claim that they were called to the profession they practice. It is not entirely clear what Louis Menand means by the term in this context. We wonder whether what the term means for him might better be expressed as indoctrination or training, both of them illiberal academic pursuits. Notice also the slightly negative connotation the term has when he says (para. 2) that permitting early entry into a field of concentration "smacks of vocationalism," as though it were a vulgar or otherwise bad thing to permit such early entry.

In teaching this essay we think we would get things going by quoting from paragraph 6, where Menand says, "The Deweyan answer . . . would be that you cannot teach people a virtue by requiring them to read books about it." Exactly why do we require students to read certain books?

For us, the most important part of Menand's essay is his final paragraph, with his comment about John Dewey and with his observation that teachers play a role far beyond their role as teachers of particular subjects.

20
Hydraulic Fracturing: Is Fracking Worth the Environmental Cost? (p. 538)

Don Carns Jr.

Shale Drilling Is a Disaster Waiting to Happen (p. 538)

The opening paragraph (beginning "I will be direct and to the point") presents the writer as, well, as someone who is direct and to the point. No nonsense here, no elaborate windup, no fancy rhetoric (in the negatives sense of the word), just (so Carns suggests) straight talk, though of course the student of rhetoric understands that this presentation of the self is in fact a rhetorical strategy, the establishment of an engaging *ethos*.

Carns goes on to present some technical material, but he is careful not to use technical terms; nothing here will cause readers to scratch their heads and mumble to themselves, "I don't understand what he is talking about." Of course he may be wrong, wrong, wrong—and that's what the next essay claims, but we do think that to the uninformed viewer, Carns comes across pretty well.

Scott Cline

Unfounded Fears about Shale Gas Obscure Facts (p. 541)

Like Carns—the essayist whom he is rebutting—Cline comes across as a guy who can be counted on to speak clearly and truthfully.

His first sentence accuses Cline of being "long on fiction and short on facts," and in his second paragraph Cline playfully re-creates the alleged fiction, a combination of the Gothic novel and sci-fi: "vast mysterious subterranean cave systems . . . [with] radioactive material in drinking water." He then returns to the present, and to his own voice, "Geez, where do I begin to correct this fictional nonsense?"

Our own impression is that Cline is knowledgeable; certainly he is confident that the facts speak for themselves. For example, he says

> Also, radioactive shale cuttings cannot hurt anyone. The extra radioactivity that people might obtain by standing next to a pile of Marcellus or Utica shale cutting is insignificantly small compared with the dose that we naturally receive from cosmic radiation, our environment, and even the food we eat.

> And radioactivity is not a threat to our drinking water. All water that returns to the surface is reused, injected, or treated so that drinking water maintains the mandated standards.

The writer of this comment on Cline's letter does not have the faintest idea if Cline is correct, but the writer also believes that Cline couldn't be saying these things if they weren't at least more or less true, true in general. And of course Cline *does* grant that there are at least *some* bad side effects of fracking, though he insists these are minor. The strategy here is venerable: Admit some weaknesses, and thus the writer gains the reader's trust that the writer sees both sides and is offering an informed opinion. What does Cline grant?

> In reality shale gas exploration boils down to a temporary traffic nuisance that can be solved by working with local communities to minimize short-term inconveniences and making sure that the water that returns to the surface through the wellbore is properly stored, transported, and either recycled or treated.

This assertion may or may not be true, but we do think it is an effective piece of writing.

Aubrey K. McClendon

Is Hydraulic Fracturing Good for the Economy? Pro (p. 542)

McClendon begins by citing a study done by Pennsylvania Sate University, presumably an impartial work. Obviously, if he had cited a study done by the gas industry, readers would be suspicious and would be unconvinced by findings that claimed fracking would bring great wealth to the area and that it had no downside. In short, McClendon begins effectively, citing an authority that the reader presumably trusts even though the reader has little or no knowledge of Penn State (other than its football team) and has not looked at the report.

Our first question in the text makes the point that McClendon originally delivered the material as a talk, probably with visual aids. In a small way, the bullets in his published essay are a sort of visual persuasion. In the text, we ask about the effect of bullets, especially compared with, say, a numbered list. It is our belief that bullets add a punchiness, a vigor, to the material that a numbered list (or a lettered list) does not have.

Our third question asks about McClendon's final paragraph, which we reproduce here:

> And remind me, what value [have] these shale gas protestors created? What jobs have they created? You know the answer, and so do I, and it's time that we contrast what we do for a living [versus] what they do for a living.

It is hard-hitting, heavily ironic: McClendon does not expect an answer when he asks his question "And remind me, what value [have] these gas protestors created?" And his original audience—presumably businessmen and engineers—must have congratulated themselves when they compared their jobs with those of the protestors. Unfortunately, we have no idea about who the protestors were—maybe students and their do-nothing, idle, highbrow professors. In any case, in its context, these final contemptuous words probably worked very well, but in print, addressed to the solitary reader, they make an impression that must be quite different from what was intended.

Jannette M. Barth

Is Hydraulic Fracturing Good for the Economy? Con (p. 544)

In her first paragraph Barth makes a distinction between capital-intensive industries (e.g., oil and gas industries, industries that require an immense amount of money, for instance for equipment, but that do not require hordes of workers) and labor-intensive industries (she doesn't give an example, but an extreme example would be a major law office, which requires lots of lawyers—people filling jobs—but very little money other than to pay for furnishings and rent).

Barth goes on to argue that the vision of drilling as a sort of money tree that will make everyone rich is a fantasy. There are *costs*, she insists, such as damage to highways, loss of revenue from hunters and tourists, and so on. Incidentally, in paragraph 3, when Barth cites some areas that will be losers, she says:

> Examples of industries likely to be negatively affected include agriculture, tourism, organic farming, wine making, hunting, fishing and river recreation.

Isn't this list a bit padded? Doesn't "agriculture" *include* "organic farming" and maybe "wine making," too, and perhaps "tourism" includes a good deal of "river recreation." Still, we do see Barth's point: One cannot just count the dollars that roll in. Further proof of some of the world's wisest words, "There is no such thing as a free lunch."

21
Drugs: Should Their Sale and Use Be Legalized? (p. 546)

Background

Next to AIDS, drugs—their use and abuse and the costs of the efforts to control them—may well be the nation's most publicized if not its most pressing social problem. Unlike AIDS, however, drug use leaves few of the users dead; and many of those who do die from drugs do not do so from overdosing or suicide, but from shoot-outs in turf wars and busted deals. The four essays we present take several divergent views of the problem and its solution.

In his inaugural address early in 1989, President George H. W. Bush reassured the nation by declaring "This scourge will end." A few months later, in a special broadcast on the drug problem, he reported that although "23 million Americans were using drugs" regularly in 1985, that number had dropped in 1988 by "almost 9 million." The president credited this gain to his administration's four-point campaign: tougher penalties, more effective enforcement, expanded treatment programs, and education to reach the young who had not yet started to use drugs. An enthusiastic elaboration of the government's efforts is presented in the articles we reprint by William J. Bennett, the nation's first drug czar (a good guy, not to be confused with a "drug kingpin," who is a bad guy), and by James Q. Wilson.

Others are more skeptical. Here are some of the disturbing facts reported in a review article, "What Ever Happened to the 'War on Drugs'?" by Michael Massing in the June 11, 1992, issue of the *New York Review of Books*.

> How many people are using illegal drugs and how frequently? According to a 2008 household survey reported by the National Institute of Drug Abuse, some 20.1 million of us used such drugs within a month prior to the survey.

What about treatment for those who want to shake the drug habit? During President Reagan's first term (again relying on data provided by Michael Massing in his survey), funds for treatment centers (adjusted for inflation) dropped by nearly 40 percent. During Reagan's second term, when crack cocaine reached epidemic proportions in the nation's inner cities, treatment centers were overwhelmed. Both the numbers of those seeking help and the extent of the treatment they needed had grown enormously. With the cocaine-related death of college basketball star Len Bias fresh on everyone's mind, the Bush administration approved a budget of $1.6 billion for treatment centers run by the states, an increase of 50 percent over the funds provided by his predecessor. But even this increase failed to meet the demand for treatment.

Turning from the issues of salience and success in the war on drugs, what is it costing us? In a 1990 article by Ethan Nadelmann, "Should Some Illegal Drugs Be Legalized?" in *Issues in Science and Technology*, we are told that the nation spent $10 billion to enforce our drug laws in 1987, perhaps twice that amount in 1990. Between 40 percent and 50 percent of all felony convictions are for drug offenses. In 1989 alone, "between three-quarters of a million and a million people were arrested . . . on drug charges." To this we must add the indirect costs. International enforcement, interdiction, and domestic enforcement—all essential elements in the government's strategy—have yet to succeed. To put it simply, we need to keep two things in mind. First, we have so far failed to keep drugs from being brought into the country. All the drugs illegal in this country and in wide use nevertheless (opium and heroin, cannabis, coca and cocaine) are native to many foreign countries and are a major cash crop in much of the world. Second, we have not succeeded in drying up demand despite granting substantial resources to law enforcement to do so.

Literature on the drug problem continues to roll off the presses; of the five books in Massing's review survey, we recommend especially *The Search for Rational Drug Control* (1992) by Franklin E. Zimring and Gordon Hawkins, an author team highly regarded for their shelf of books on virtually every problem in criminal justice.

William J. Bennett

Drug Policy and the Intellectuals (p. 546)

William J. Bennett gives a vigorous defense of the national drug policy he was assigned to carry out by the first Bush administration. He attacks intellectuals (the only two he names are the liberal columnist Anthony Lewis and the conservative spokesman William F. Buckley Jr. in para. 8; but he alludes to a host of unnamed "prominent residents" on the campuses of Princeton, Wisconsin, Harvard, and Stanford in para. 18) for their faults in blinding themselves and the nation to the evils of legalizing drug use, a policy supported (he says) by "a series of superficial and even disingenuous ideas" (para. 8).

Here's a quick summary of Bennett's seven-point argument against the legalization of drugs (question 3): (1) Criminalizing drugs provides an incentive to stay out of the business (para. 10); (2) no one has figured out how to carry out a policy of legalization of drugs across the board, from marijuana to PCP (para. 11); (3) if drugs are legalized, their use will "soar" (para. 13), thereby increasing the harm and suffering to the users; (4) the cost to the nation of more drug use would be "intolerably high" (para. 14); (5) drug-related crimes would not decrease at all (para. 15); (6) the terrible problems we have with legalized alcohol are a foretaste of the even graver problems we would have were all drugs legalized (para. 16); (7) apart from all the foregoing, "heavy drug use destroys character," "dignity and autonomy" (para. 17). We have to admit Bennett makes a pretty convincing argument, spiced with barbs at "America's pundits and academic cynics" along the way.

Were someone to accuse Bennett of hypocrisy or inconsistency (question 4), he might well reply in the same manner that he does regarding legalization of alcohol (para. 16): No doubt it would be a futile effort for society now to make tobacco use illegal; yet he would be better off (as he might well admit) if he had never acquired the nicotine habit and if he could get rid of it. But whether he can is his personal medical problem; there is no inconsistency in his urging a policy to the effect that everyone (himself included) avoid harmful illegal drugs, even if he is unable to cease using a harmful legal drug himself. Of course, he might also take another line, that nicotine addiction is not as harmful as addiction to any illegal drug. But that is an empirical claim, and it is far from clear whether it is true.

James Q. Wilson

Against the Legalization of Drugs (p. 553)

This essay following William J. Bennett's reminds us of the "good cop/bad cop" routine in police interrogation. We debated whether to include both these essays, since the argument in each is pretty much the same. But the tone is so different — James Q. Wilson thoughtful and patient, Bennett using words as though they were clubs — that we thought this difference itself is worth some reflection. (Students might well be set the task of reading these two essays as a pair and explaining what, if anything, is different in the two arguments and, that apart, which essay has the more persuasive, effective tone.)

The idea of "victimless crimes" (our question 1) gained prominence in the 1960s, as part of an argument for decriminalizing various drug and sex offenses, as well as gambling. When consenting adults engage in illegal practices that harm no one (or harm only themselves), so the argument went, they have committed a victimless crime. But such acts ought to be decriminalized because the criminal law in such cases is improperly invading privacy, liberty, and autonomy. (John Stuart Mill made this argument famous, although he did not use the term *victimless crimes*.) Wilson seems to object to this argument on two grounds (para. 24). First, he rejects the criterion of state intervention as too narrow: "Society is not and could never be," he says, "a collection of autonomous individuals." So we need the criminal law here and there for admittedly paternalistic purposes. Consequently, even if drug abuse were a victimless crime, Wilson might not approve of its legalization. Second, he rejects the factual minor premise of the victimless crime argument; drug use is harmful not only to the user but also to others who have not or cannot consent (there is "fetal drug syndrome," for example).

Wilson is a skillful, polished arguer, and we draw attention to some of these features of his essay in two of our questions (the second and the fourth). The "economic dilemma" that the drug legalizers face, to which Wilson refers in his paragraph 37 (our fourth question), can be formulated somewhat more briefly than he does, as follows: Tax money from legalized drugs will pay for the cost of regulation and treatment of users, abusers, and addicts, or it will not. If it does, then the tax rate on drugs must be set quite high, but this will lead to tax evasion and crime and a black market in drugs. If tax money from drugs does not fully finance the costs of regulation and treatment, then we will have more addicts and either inadequately financed treatment centers or less tax money for other public needs. But none of these alternatives is acceptable. Therefore, we cannot reasonably legalize drugs in the expectation that taxing them (as alcohol and tobacco are now taxed) will enable society to pay for the costs.

Like any dilemma worthy of the name (see our discussion of the dilemma in the text), this one has a disjunctive tautology as its major premise (that is, the premise states two exhaustive and exclusive alternatives). Such a premise is invulnerable to criticism. Criticism can be directed, however, at each of the two other conditional premises ("if . . . , then . . ."), as they are empirical generalizations and vulnerable on factual grounds. Or criticism can be focused on the premise that expresses how unacceptable the dilemma is. Perhaps one of these alternatives is not so bad after all, especially when compared with the costs of losing the war on drugs. One way to develop that thought would be by constructing a counterdilemma, showing the awkward consequences of *not* legalizing drugs. (Here, we leave that task for another day.)

In his criticism of Nadelmann (paras. 25–26), Wilson accuses him of "a logical fallacy and a factual error." The fallacy is to infer (1) the percentage of occasional cocaine users who become "binge users" when the drug is *legal* from (2) the percentage who become "binge users" when (as at present) the drug is *illegal*. Why does Wilson think this is a fallacy? To be sure, (1) and (2) are quite independent propositions, and it is possible that the percentage of users would grow (rather than stay roughly constant, as Nadelmann infers) as soon as the drug is legalized. But by how much? At what rate? In the face of antidrug education? These unanswered questions apart, what Wilson needs to show us is that in general, or perhaps in some closely parallel case, the number of those who do X when doing X is illegal has no relationship to the number of those who do X when doing X is legal. But Wilson hasn't shown this at all.

As for the "factual error," it looks to us as though Wilson has caught Nadelmann in an error (see para. 27).

Milton Friedman

There's No Justice in the War on Drugs (p. 567)

Milton Friedman was the nation's best-known free-market economist and the author of many books, including *Capitalism and Freedom* (1962). He and his fellow conservatives seem to be divided over the nation's "war on drugs." Some, like William J. Bennett, strongly favor fighting the use of illegal drugs with unrelenting fervor. Others, believing that drug use harms only or principally the user, oppose government interference (either in the form of regulation or outright prohibition) and favor using free-market methods to control its use. Friedman is of the latter persuasion. He hints at reasons of this sort in his paragraph 2, where he quotes himself from 1972. There, in a phrase, his position was this: Persuasion, yes; coercion, no.

What is surprising about Friedman's essay is that he does not rely on free-market reasoning. It's not that he rejects such reasoning; it's rather that he invokes what he describes as "ethical" considerations of several different sorts. They constitute a variety of objections, each of which represents one kind of empirical consequence of the policy of the past four decades but inadequately foreseen when the war on drugs was launched with much fanfare by President Nixon in 1972.

Regarding question 1, here is one way the thesis of his essay might be stated in a sentence: "The unethical consequences of the nation's war on drugs far outweigh whatever advantages have been or might be gained." (This version is inspired by the rhetorical question Friedman asks at the end of his essay, in para. 12.)

As to question 2 (and also question 4), an "expediential" objection to the war on drugs would be any claim that its harmful consequences (for example, in tempting the police into corruption) outweigh its good consequences. A moral (or ethical) objection would be that our drug policies violate some moral norm, standard, or principle (for example, the principle that adults ought to be left free of governmental interference to act as they wish — including using drugs — so long as they do not harm others).

Elliott Currie

Toward a Policy on Drugs (p. 570)

Elliott Currie's position on the drug controversy (our question 4) includes three steps: (1) move toward decriminalizing the drug user (but not necessarily the trafficker), (2) treat marijuana (use as well as dealing?) "differently" from (he means more leniently than) "the harder drugs" (mainly heroin and cocaine, we surmise), and (3) permit medical experimentation with certain drugs (which ones he does not say, but marijuana is the obvious example) (para. 18). These recommendations (all adopted in one way or another, he says, by "some European countries") fall well short of radical decriminalization of drugs, but if Currie is right, to go any further is to cause predictable costs and harms that make radical decriminalization the wrong social policy.

Is Currie convincing that these steps, and these only, are a reasonable compromise between those who want to carry on the "war on drugs" no matter what the costs and those who want all aspects of drug use, sale, and manufacture to be permitted by law? (He presented these views over two decades ago, and we suspect he would say today that precious little progress has been made over this period to bring any of these three recommendations to come to pass.) We do not have a better proposal to offer, and we think at the very least that his middle way between the two extremes deserves careful thought. The prospect of ideas such as his receiving careful thought at the highest levels in our governments, state and federal, are not encouraging.

In our question 2 we mention three possible steps to reduce the role of drugs in our lives, steps Currie does not mention. Why doesn't he? As a guess, we suggest this. He would reject our first suggestion (curbing manufacture of illegal drugs) because either most of the drugs in question are not manufactured in the United States or the one that mainly is (marijuana) he wants largely to decriminalize. Perhaps he would reject our second suggestion (reducing imports of illegal drugs) on the grounds that federal agencies have tried for years to do precisely this but to little effect and that tax dollars to curb heavy drug importing can be more effectively spent elsewhere. As for our third suggestion (aggressive public education), perhaps he could argue it is implicit and is presupposed in much of what he says.

The evident uniqueness of the magnitude of the drug problem in this country troubles us. Currie mentions the issue (para. 21), but he offers no explanation for our unfortunate plight. We mention (question 5) three possible explanations that seem to us unconvincing. We don't have a fourth to offer for contemplation. So long as there is no convincing and generally accepted explanation, it seems likely to us that the drug problem will not abate. Meanwhile, the human cost in our drug policies ought to terrify and infuriate. In New York, for example, drug laws enacted during the Rockefeller administration (as reported by the Fortune Society) mandate a fifteen-years-to-life sentence for the sale of two ounces or the possession of four ounces of an illegal drug. Is there any convincing reason why our society ought to persist in enacting and enforcing such laws? We earnestly doubt it.

22
Junk Food: Should the Government Regulate Our Intake? (p. 581)

Anonymous Editorial

New York Times (p. 582)

Adopting a fairly common argumentative strategy, the opening paragraph speaks well of a proponent of the view that the essay will oppose. And then, having shown its goodwill, the essay turns to attacking the proponent's proposal.

The reversal comes early in the second paragraph, with *however*, the third word in the paragraph. The third and fourth paragraphs make it clear that the editorial is not merely negative and is not merely going to say that the mayor should mind his own business, that government should leave people alone, and so on. Rather, these paragraphs offer suggestions about what the mayor's office *should* be doing. The approach, then, is not at all along libertarian lines. Quite the opposite: The government is encouraged to educate the public "to make sound choices," and thus it should "keep up its tough anti-obesity advertising campaigns" (para. 4).

The final paragraph suggest, in fact, that the trouble with "nannying" is that it might have the reverse effect; that is, it "might well cause people to tune out."

Anonymous

Pictorial Advertisement, The Nanny (p. 584)

The ad was sponsored by the Center for Consumer Freedom, an organization established in 1995 with funds from Philip Morris. In 1995, the center's cause was opposition to attempts to curb smoking in restaurants, but it now engages in a variety of actions on behalf of the fast-food, alcohol, and tobacco industries.

The ad shows a photo-shopped image of Mayor Bloomberg in a purple button-down knit dress, hunched but towering over a toylike New York City skyline. Large letters at the top identify the figure as "The Nanny," and in case we miss the point, smaller letters at the bottom of the image say, "New Yorkers need a Mayor, not a Nanny." And in between, some text tells us that "Nanny Bloomberg has taken his strange obsession with what you eat one step further."

Is the image amusing? Answers will vary. Some viewers may say that this image, showing a man wearing a funny-looking woman's outfit, standing in a funny position with his knees together, ridicules not only Bloomberg but (when you think a moment about it) also ridicules nannies, that is, ridicules women who devote their lives to the strenuous and important task of supervising children. And these viewers, or others, may point out that although the ad speaks of "Nanny Bloomberg's strange obsession" with what we eat, one cannot get through the day without seeing in the newspaper or hearing on radio or TV something about the dire effects of obesity in the United States, notably its connection to heart disease and to Type 2 diabetes. Lots of people (not just the mayor and his subordinates) are talking about lots of illness, lots of death, lots of physical and mental suffering, and lots of money—money spent on unhealthful foods, and money spent on consequent medical treatment. These people are not behaving ridiculously.

Daniel E. Lieberman

Evolution's Sweet Tooth (p. 585)

When the anti-Bloomberg advertisement (text, p. 584) asks, "What's next? Limits on the width of a slice of pizza . . .?" it is introducing the kind of argument that has been called "the slippery slope." (We discuss this kind of thinking—this kind of fallacy— in the text, p. 372.) Lieberman raises the issue in his first paragraph, rightly saying that this libertarian objection deserves attention, and his essential argument turns out to be yes, we *should* go beyond sugary drinks, *should* descend the slope—and we *do* need a nanny; that is, we need authoritative enforcement. Here is how he puts it in his second paragraph:

> Lessons from evolutionary biology support the mayor's plan: when it comes to limiting sugar in our food, some kinds of coercive action are not only necessary but also consistent with how we used to live.

"Coercive action"!!! Why? and How? we may well ask. And Lieberman tells us—first by sketching the biological background that has caused this problem of obesity, and then by sketching possible courses of action—*why* coercion is not only necessary but also consistent. The possible courses of action, he says in paragraphs 7–9, are these:

- Do nothing.

- Rely on education.

- Collectively restore our diets to a more natural state through regulations.

"Regulations" of course mean laws, which gets us back to libertarian objections. Lieberman grants that the Bloomberg proposal is paternalistic (the male version of nannyism). But he insists that it "is not an aberrant form of coercion," and it is (he says in para. 9) "a very small step toward restoring a natural part of our environment." And who, one might ask, can argue against restoring what is "natural"? One might ask, however, is it indeed "a very small step" or is it the first paternalistic step down a slippery slope?

In paragraphs 10 and 11 Lieberman argues—surely he is correct—that we *are* paternalistic with children:

> Youngsters can't make rational, informed decisions about their bodies, and our society agrees that parents don't have the right to make disastrous decisions on their behalf. Accordingly, we require parents to enroll their children in school, have them immunized, and make them wear seat belts. We . . . don't let children buy alcohol or cigarettes. If these are acceptable forms of coercion, how is restricting unhealthy doses of sugary drinks that slowly contribute to disease any different?

If you read these sentences in class, a lively discussion will follow.

Mark Bittman

Bad Food? Tax It, and Subsidize Vegetables (p. 587)

Bittman begins his argument with a time-tested formula: He calls our attention to a problem. And, to further engage our interest—in effect, to assure us that he is a writer we will enjoy reading—he includes a bit of word play (the business about SAD, at the end of the first paragraph). And, while we are mentioning SAD, we can here call attention to the fact that he *ends* the essay by returning to the Standard American Diet, which is to say that he, like most professional authors, provides a structural model that students might well emulate.

In his fourth paragraph he offers a reason why we cannot count on the food industry to provide healthful food, and so, he says, the federal government should intervene "as an agent of the public good." In the view of the sponsors of the anti-Bloomberg advertisement that we reproduce in the text on page 584, such intervention is nannyism, but as Lieberman points out in his essay, everyone (or almost everyone) agrees that nannyism is sometimes appropriate when we are dealing with youngsters. For instance, we do not let them buy alcohol or tobacco.

The fifth paragraph points out that the government does already meddle in the food industry: It *subsidizes* certain crops—so why (Bittman argues) should we not tax unhealthful crops? The tax would (para. 7) reduce the consumption of unhealthful foods, and the revenue could be used to subsidize (and thus bring down the price of) healthful food, a win/win situation.

In his ninth paragraph Bittman grants that this proposal would of course upset the processed food industry, and it would also upset the consumers of such goods because the prices of such things (e.g., soda and chips) would be increased. But his response is that "public health is the role of the government." (The libertarians may have a different view.)

"The benefits are staggering," he tells us in paragraph 19, and "the need is dire" (para. 20). (Libertarians will not agree.) "Education alone is no match for marketing dollars that push the very foods that are the worst for us" (para. 20). In paragraph 21 he cites $344 billion as the projected health cost of obesity in 2018—a figure that may well urge a reader to think sympathetically about a tax on those who help to generate this cost. In order to support his proposal, he cites "the historic 1998 tobacco settlement" (para. 22), which undoubtedly has resulted in a substantial decrease in smoking and thereby immense medical savings. And in paragraph 25 he again refers to the successful campaign against smoking, the idea being that history supports his proposal.

23
Facebook: How Has Social Networking Changed How We Relate to Others? (p. 594)

Lauren Tarshis

Is Facebook Making You Mean? (p. 594)

We think that almost all of the essays in our book are well-written, and that in some degree they can serve as models for students. That is, instructors can invite students to look at *how* the authors go about their business of developing arguments: What does this open-ing paragraph *do*, why does the author define this term but not that term, why does the author devote two paragraphs to this point but only one paragraph to that point? When we do this sort of thing in class, we are in effect saying, "See what is going on in these essays, see how writers go about their business. You find this writing effective. Now try to get some of *that* into your own writing."

Tarshis's essay seems to us to lend itself to such an approach. After all, she does not bring to the topic any highly specialized knowledge that the student cannot possibly have. True, she quotes a source or two and occasionally says something like "Experts say," but the meat and potatoes of the essay is in her presentation of material available to all of us. Thus, when she is making the point (para. 14) that online communication deprives us of clues that are available with other forms of communication, she gives some very good examples:

> One of the most important ways in which we communicate with each other is through subtle emotional signals—your best friend's blush when you mention a girl he likes, the flash of anger in your mother's eyes when you say you'll take out the garbage *later*. Over the phone we can hear a change in a person's tone, or the ominous pause that sends a message to back off. Online communication takes all of these signals away.

The basic point—that communication is not just words, but consists also of "subtle emotional signals"—is made clear and memorable by the *details* that Tarshis provides, and these details are not based on esoteric information that students cannot reasonably be supposed to be familiar with.

The end of her essay—two paragraphs, the second of which consists of only two words—also seems to us to be worth discussing in class. Ordinarily of course one would *not* end with a two-word paragraph, but here it is effective—for reasons that students will easily see *if* you ask them to discuss it.

Steven Levy

Facebook Reset (p. 596)

Levy adopts a highly informal tone—notice the contraction in his first sentence ("didn't"), the beginning of the second sentence ("After all"), and the use of "pretty much" in his third sentence. None of these things is surprising, since the piece originally appeared in *Wired*—not, for instance, in a book published by the University of Chicago Press. We find Levy's writing engaging; we do not think he descends into vulgarity, or that he is nudging us in the ribs. A reader never doubts that Levy is a competent writer and is well-informed about his topic. His second paragraph, for instance, begins thus: "The list is the gateway through which people observe our major life events, causal musings, physical peregrinations, and crop yields on FarmVille." Our point? We think it is worth calling attention to Levy's tone: By observing it, students can learn that a writer can be informal and at the same time can convey authority.

We confess that we wrote the preceding paragraph a few hours after one of our colleagues told us that he *never* allows students to use the first-person singular pronoun. We doubt that we want to see it in an undergraduate honors essay on, say, "Orwell's Use of Metaphor as a Persuasive Device" (except in the Preface), but we certainly think it can be used in college writing that is directed at the general reader.

Speaking of metaphor, we want to call attention to Levy's effective metaphor in his third paragraph, where he says that his Facebook collection of friends "resembles the contents of a house occupied by a hoarder." He goes on:

> I make my way past heaps of classmates, overfriendly PR people, and folks whose amusing conversations in hotel bars led to morning-after friend requests. Open a closet and out tumble a Chinese poet, sources from stories I wrote for now-defunct publications, and one of my son's high-school friends with whom he hasn't spoken in years. Trying the front door, I trip over the mashup artist Girl Talk, whom I met once in Pittsburgh. Meanwhile, many of my best friends and closest business contacts aren't even in the house.

In several places in our book, and in this manual, we claim that students can learn to *write* by studying the writing of others. That is, students can learn the importance of an engaging (or at least a clear) title, of an opening paragraph that does not merely repeat the title, of transitions that help the reader to see where the author is going, and so on, but we do confess that some aspects of good writing probably cannot be taught—and one of these is the use of metaphor. Here is Aristotle (in the *Poetics*) on the subject:

> But the greatest thing by far is to have a command of metaphor. This alone cannot be imparted by another; it is the mark of genius, for to make good metaphors implies an eye for resemblances. (1459a4)

Still, even if we cannot teach students how to invent metaphor, we can at least alert them to perceive it in what they read—and to enjoy it. Levy's final paragraph, with its use of "Mulligan" (a second chance to make a move in a game) is, in its smaller way, another use of metaphor that is probably beyond most of us—certainly, it is beyond the inventive power of the writer of this comment—but it is worth calling to the attention of students, with the aim of helping them to see that reading can be fun.

Jenna Wortham

It's Not about You, Facebook, It's about Us (p. 598)

We don't think this essay can cause any readers any difficulties. For us, the chief interest is whether our students will find it true. That is, does this business (see especially para. 7–8) about not knowing how to live *with* Facebook and how to live *without* it correspond to the experience of students? Students may offer plenty of examples confirming Wortham's assertion that there really is an issue—or, on the other hand, maybe they won't.

If you do assign the essay and ask for a written response, we suggest that you caution your students to make certain that their essay has a *point* (a thesis) and an organization, so that it is not simply a string of anecdotes ("This happened, and that happened, and then another thing happened").

The piece was written early in 2012, so it ought to reflect current thinking.

Stephen Marche

Is Facebook Making Us Lonely? (p. 600)

It seems to us that it takes Marche a while to get there, but his final answer to the question he poses in his title is, in effect, "No, it is really doing something worse. It has produced a new kind of isolation. We spend an inordinate amount of time with the Internet and thus we neglect our connection with the real world. [Why the Internet is not part of the real world is unclear to the writer of this comment.] Our alleged obsession with the Internet deprives us of the opportunity to 'forget about ourselves for a while.'"

Our third question asks about Marche's reference (para. 17) to "social capital," a term that we assume will be unfamiliar to most first-year students. *Capital* is wealth—dollars, real money—used for the production of more wealth (e.g., dollars that are invested); *social capital* is another sort of wealth, not dollars that produce more dollars but social connections (*social* is ultimately from the Latin word *socius*, "companion") that produce wealth. Examples: a friend who helps you to get a job or a promotion or who buys a product you are selling. In short, if a person's contacts, connections, network can generate money (presumably because the friends *trust* the individual), that person possesses "social capital." While we are talking about forms of capital, we add, almost irrelevantly, that a college degree can be considered "educational capital."

Marche cites many studies, or, more precisely, he mentions many studies but sometimes he gives little information about how to identify them. For example, in para. 8, he speaks with a maddening lack of specificity about "A 2005 analysis of data from a longitudinal study of Dutch twins." It is our guess that many readers may be skeptical of such studies. Possibly we are reflecting only our own skepticism, our own distrust of sociological surveys, but we think that many readers may believe that their own responses, their own perceptions of loneliness, are better guides than are the statistical surveys of such topics as "family loneliness" (see our fourth question).

Josh Rose

How Social Media Is Having a Positive Impact on Our Culture (p. 612)

This essay—like many essays discussing Facebook—is highly personal. It is hard for us to imagine an essayist of, say, even ten years ago (to say nothing of an essayist of the generation of George Orwell) writing such sentences as (para. 2):

> First, on my way to go sit down and read the newspaper at my coffee shop, I got a message from my 10-year-old son, just saying good morning and letting me know he was going to a birthday party today. I don't get to see him all the time. He's growing up in two houses, as I did.

Of course a decade ago ten-year-olds were not sending messages to their fathers, and even if they were, their fathers would not think such messages were worth talking about to other adults. But today, as the presence of our casebook indicates, messaging is a hot topic. And we have tried to choose notably interesting essays on this topic. Still, we must confess that as we scanned dozens of essays in order to find a few for our casebook, we often felt that (to adapt Rose's fourth paragraph) one man's treasure is another man's TMI.

Our second question in the text invites students to talk—rather, to write—about *how* they use new media. Our hope, we confess, is that they will report, sure, they have fun with it, but they also use it to get access to information and that helps them to become better human beings.

24
Immigration: What Is to Be Done? (p. 615)

Background

Before looking at David Cole's article, we will (1) give some history and (2) survey the chief arguments for and against keeping the gate open.

In 1924, the law provided a national-origins quota system that favored northern and western Europe and severely restricted immigration from everywhere else. This system was replaced in 1965 by a law (with amendments) that said there were three reasons to award visas to immigrants:

1. An immigrant might possess certain job skills, especially skills that this country needs. (Relatively few visas were awarded on this basis.)

2. An immigrant might be a refugee from war or from political persecution and so eligible for "political asylum."

3. An immigrant might be related to an American citizen or to a legal alien (the "family reunification policy").

In 1965, when this policy was formulated, there was little immigration from Latin America, the Caribbean, and Asia. Today, 90 percent of all immigration to the United States comes from those areas. Upward of 80 percent are people of color. Whatever our policy is, it is *not* racist. What about numbers, rather than percentages? The peak decade for immigration was 1901 to 1910, when about 8.7 million immigrants arrived, chiefly from southern and eastern Europe. Some authorities say that 1981 to 1990 matched this, if illegal immigrants are included; but in any case, in 1901 to 1910, the total U.S. population was less than one-third of what it is today. After 1910, immigration declined sharply; in all of the 1930s, only about 500,000 immigrants came to the United States, and in all of the 1940s, there were only about 1 million including refugees from Nazi persecution. The figure now is about 1.5 million annually, plus an unknown number of illegal immigrants (the usual guess is half a million annually). Of illegal immigrants in the United States in 2005, 6 percent came from Canada and Europe, 13 percent from Asia, 56 percent from Mexico, 22 percent from elsewhere in Latin America, and 3 percent from Africa and elsewhere.

What about ethnic identity in the recent past, from 1880 onward? When Nathan Glazer and Daniel Patrick Moynihan wrote *Beyond the Melting Pot* (1963), they found that the ethnic groups that had arrived between 1880 and 1920 retained their identities. Will Herberg, in *Protestant, Catholic, Jew* (rev. ed. 1960), found that at best there was a "triple melting pot"—that is, people married outside their ethnic groups but still within their religious groups. Thus, Italian Americans for the most part married Catholics, but these Catholics might be Irish; similarly, German Jews married Jews, but they might be Russian Jews. From 1980 onward, however, religious identity too was shaken. For instance, half of all Italian Americans born after World War II married non-Catholics; 40 percent of Jews marrying in the 1980s married Gentiles (according to Robert C. Christopher, *Crashing the Gates* [1989]).

In selecting material for our text, we read fairly widely, and we noticed that certain arguments kept recurring. Because instructors may find it useful to have the chief arguments on both sides, we list them. Please understand that we are not endorsing any of these arguments; we are just reporting them.

Arguments in Favor
of a Relatively Open Door

1. *Immigrants provide cheap labor and do not displace native-born workers.* Immigrants work as gardeners, farm laborers, domestic helpers, restaurant employees, and so on. They do not displace American workers, since Americans (white and African American) will not take these jobs at the current wages. True, Americans *would* take the jobs if the pay were higher—a majority of the people who do jobs such as domestic work, agricultural labor, taxi driving, and valet parking are Americans, not immigrants—but the fact is, the pay is low, and *in areas where there are a great many immigrants* the wages are very low and Americans reject the jobs.

   But, again, it is argued that immigrants do not displace American workers. In 1980 the Mariel boatlift brought 125,000 Cubans, increasing Miami's workforce by 7 percent virtually overnight, but it had no effect on the wages of skilled or unskilled labor, black or white. Further, job losses are more than offset by new jobs generated by immigrants; after all, immigrants need housing, food, and so on, and therefore they are a new market.

2. *Immigrants provide high-tech knowledge.* Silicon Valley depends largely on immigrant engineers, microchip designers, and so on.

3. *Immigrants stimulate the economy.* Many immigrants have founded companies, thereby generating thousands of jobs.

4. *Immigrants are assimilating at the usual rate.* Despite assertions that immigrants today are not assimilating, they are in fact assimilating in pretty much the same ways that their predecessors did. Their children marry outside the group (in California, nearly half of the native-born Asians and Latinos marry into other ethnic groups), their grandchildren often do not know the language of the immigrants, and so on. The charge that immigrants do not assimilate is an old one; for instance, it was regularly said of the Irish in the nineteenth century.

5. *Immigrants are not a threat to the peace of the cities.* San Jose, California, is the eleventh-largest city in the United States, with a white population less than 50 percent, but it has the lowest murder and robbery rates of any major city in the United States, and it has virtually no ethnic conflict. El Paso is 70 percent Latino, but it has one of the lowest rates of serious crime or murder; the robbery rate is one-half that of Seattle, an overwhelmingly white city of similar size. Hawaii, too—the state with the lowest percentage of whites in the United States—has a low rate for serious crime and little ethnic conflict.

6. *Immigrants may cost us something in the short run, but in the long run they add to the country.* They are energetic workers, increasing the supply of goods and services with their labor, and increasing the demand for goods and services by spending their wages. Refugees—the immigrant group that gains the most public sympathy—are the immigrants who cost the government the most in welfare and in Medicaid.

7. *Immigrants from developing societies are likely to have strong family structures.* We fret that immigrants from developing nations are likely to be poorer and less well educated than those from Europe, but they come from traditional societies with strong moral codes. The collapse of family values originated not with the arrival of Haitians, but in the white Anglo communities, where, for instance, in 2001, 22.5 percent of the children were born out of wedlock.

8. *We are a nation of immigrants; our strength is derived from our openness to all cultures.* The fear of immigrants is now in large measure a fear of cultures new to the United States, and a fear of persons of color. In some instances, it is rooted in hostility to what one writer calls "anti-progressive Iberian values"—that is, the values of Roman Catholic Latinos.

Arguments in Favor of Shutting the Door, or Keeping It Only Narrowly Ajar

1. *Immigrants cost the United States money.* (a) Since most immigrants are at the low end of the wage scale, and (b) since they have children of school age, they cost local governments more in services (especially education, health services, and welfare) than they pay in sales and income taxes. Moreover, (c) they constitute a disproportionate percentage of prisoners (in California, 20 percent of the prison population).

2. *Today's immigrants are not assimilating at the rate that earlier immigrants assimilated.* In the past, most immigrants came from England, Ireland, or Europe, and they were glad to put their old countries behind them. Many never returned to the countries of their birth, partly because they had no affection for those countries and partly because the trip was long and costly. Today, many Latinos fly back and forth between the United States and Central or South America, thereby keeping up their cultural ties with their countries of origin. And in fact the new emphasis on multiculturalism encourages them to retain their identities rather than to enter into the melting pot. The result is the nation's loss of a common culture, a common language.

   The culture of our country is essentially northern European and Christian. The vast increase in Latinos and Asians brings into question whether we will continue to have a national identity.

3. *Immigrants deprive Americans of jobs.* By working in substandard conditions and for substandard wages, immigrants keep wages low and they deprive citizens of jobs. In California and in Texas it is especially evident that immigrants have displaced unskilled native-born workers.

4. *Immigrants today are less skilled than those of the past.* Because they are less skilled, they are more likely to become a burden to the state.

5. *Immigration is unfair to countries from where the immigrants come.* Among the immigrants from developing nations are some who are politically dissatisfied or who are economically unfulfilled. These are precisely the people who can improve their own countries; this brain drain is unfair to those countries. (The usual reply to this is to say that such people emigrate precisely because they cannot exercise their talent in their native countries because of various obstacles.)

6. *It is nonsense to justify immigration today by saying, "We are a nation of immigrants."* First of all, most nations are nations of immigrants. For instance, England was invaded by the Vikings, by people from Germanic areas, and later by the Norman French. Even the supposedly homogeneous Japanese are believed to have experienced several waves of prehistoric immigration from Korea. Second, that immigration was good for us in the past does not mean it still is good for us. The times have changed. For instance, today the country is heavily populated and the immigrants come from different cultures.

The Two Basic Questions

Finally, it is probably appropriate to say that both sides agree there are two basic questions:

1. Which and how many immigrants ought we to take? (The usual answer to the first part of this question is, "People like me.")

2. How ought we to enforce the law—that is, what measures can reduce illegal immigration? (About 95 percent of the illegal border crossings come from Mexico—but many of these illegal entrants do not stay in this country. Further, many illegal immigrants do *not* enter surreptitiously; they enter legally, but stay beyond the time specified on their visas.)

Current answers to this second question often take the form of responding to a bill that the late Senator Arlen Specter introduced in 2006. The gist: Illegal immigrants who entered before January 7, 2004, could apply for a three-year guest-worker visa, renewable once (for another three years) if the applicant paid a $1,000 fine and cleared a background check. After six years, if the applicant showed competence in English and paid another $1,000 fine and paid back taxes, he or she could apply for citizenship.

What else to do: Today, one often hears—again, usually in response to Specter's proposal—that we should (1) erect a high wall (literal or metaphoric) (i.e., we should expand the Border Patrol), (2) strictly enforce workshop rules (i.e., severely penalize employers of undocumented workers), and (3) widen the gate (i.e., ease the pressure for visas).

The DREAM Act: An acronym for Development, Relief, and Education for Alien Minors. First introduced in the Senate in 2001, it is still much talked about. The gist, as set forth in Wikipedia, is as follows:

- Conditional permanent residency for certain undocumented residents of good moral character who

  • graduate from U.S. high schools.

  • arrived in the U.S. as minors.

  • lived here continuously for at least five years before the bill's enactment.

- If they complete two years of military service or two years at a four-year college or university, they can obtain temporary residency for a six-year period. Within the six years, they may qualify for permanent residency if they have

  "acquired a degree from an institution of higher learning in the UnitedStates, or have completed at least two years in a bachelor's degree program or higher degree program, or have served in the armed forces for at least two years and, if discharged, received an honorable discharge."

The chief arguments against the DREAM Act are that it is, in effect, amnesty, a reward for illegal immigration, and that it invites further illegal immigration.

David Cole

Five Myths about Immigration (p. 615)

David Cole's use of the word *myths* in his title suggests that he subscribes to the old adage, "The best defense is a strong offense." His basic strategy, clearly, is to say that *X, Y,* and *Z* are untrue—with the implication that his own views must therefore be true.

In the course of his opening attack he introduces the Know-Nothings (properly called the American Party), the anti-immigrant and anti-Catholic (specifically, anti-Irish) movement in the 1850s. Subgroups of secret societies formed (for example, the Order of the Star-Spangled Banner), but when members were asked awkward questions about their beliefs, they replied with a stock statement, to the effect that they knew nothing, hence the nickname.

In short, Cole begins by introducing the Know-Nothings, a most unpleasant bunch who were associated with hatred of immigrants, and he then announces that the persons he opposes subscribe not to "mistakes" or "errors," but to myths—enduring, attractive-looking falsehoods. All in all, a rhetorically effective beginning. We are surprised, however, that he does not repeat the powerful word *myths.* For instance, he could have said, "Myth No. 1," "Myth No. 2," and so on, and he could have explained why he calls them myths rather than mistakes, errors, falsehoods, or whatever.

In the third paragraph he introduces the point that he is descended from the poor Irish whom the Know-Nothings wanted to keep out, the idea being that he is a decent guy so we can see how wrong these foes of immigrants were. In the next paragraph he clarifies the point; yesterday it was the Irish, but since the Irish—"they"—have now become "us," of course, today's unwanted immigrants go by a different name. The "they" of our times, he says, "are Latin Americans (most recently, Cubans), Haitians and Arab Americans, among others."

We don't need to comment on Cole's "myths," except to say, first, that some of the things in our list of pros and cons at the beginning of this discussion may be useful in evaluating his views, and, second, in his discussion of the myth concerning the costs of immigrants (paras. 10–13), he does in fact grudgingly admit that on the local level, immigrants may cost the community money: "At most, such figures suggest that some redistribution of federal and state monies may be appropriate" (para. 11).

Let's end by returning to Cole's rhetoric. We think his final paragraph is effective. In it, he returns to the "they" versus "us" of his opening (paras. 3–4), and he more or less appeals to the decency of his readers: "I was always taught that we will be judged by how we treat others" (para. 19). The implication is that we should be decent, just, and so on, and that we do not at present treat immigrants fairly or humanely. He hasn't quite proved this—one might, for a start, insist that he could show a little more sympathy for the taxpayers in some communities (Texas and California)—but probably most readers will agree that he comes across as a decent fellow and that he has given us some things to think about.

Barry R. Chiswick

The Worker Next Door (p. 619)

We want to give a bit of background relevant to the specific issue of immigrants versus American citizens in low-paying jobs. In a recent *New York Times* article, according to the Center for Immigration Studies, "immigrants are a majority of workers in only 4 of 473 job classifications: stucco masons, tailors, produce sorters, and beauty salon workers, but even in these four categories native-born workers account for more than 40 percent of the workers." Thus, although virtually all of the grape cutters in the San Joaquin Valley are immigrants, half of all agricultural workers in the United States are native-born. Similarly, although a majority of cab drivers and valet parkers in New York City are immigrants, when viewed nationwide, cab drivers and valet parkers are mostly native-born.

On the front page of the September 22, 2006, *New York Times*, a story ran about fruit rotting in California and Washington because pickers could not be found. Here are the third and fourth paragraphs and the beginning of the fifth:

> Now harvest time has passed and tons of pears have ripened to mush on their branches, while the ground of Mr. Ivicevich's orchard reeks with rotting fruit. He and other growers in Lake county, about 90 miles north of San Francisco, could not find enough pickers.
>
> Stepped-up border enforcement kept many illegal Mexican immigrant workers out of California this year, farmers and labor contractors said, putting new strain on the state's shrinking seasonal farm labor force.
>
> Labor shortages have also been reported by apple growers in Washington and upstate New York.

Are the least-educated Americans at a disadvantage because of immigrant workers? Yes, where they compete with immigrants. But the point seems to be this: It is *not* true that there are jobs Americans will not do. What is true is that some Americans will not do these jobs when the pay is very low.

Let's look briefly at Chiswick's essay, chiefly to see what a student can learn from it about writing an argument. Chiswick begins, "It is often said that . . ." Experienced readers will expect that—pretty soon—they will get a "but." Of course it is conceivable that the writer would go on to say that what is often said is indeed true, but nine times out of ten the writer is setting up a view that he or she will reject, and that is exactly what Chiswick is doing here. The first lesson that inexperienced writers can learn from Chiswick, then, is this: The opening sentence in an essay is, so to speak, the beginning of a dramatic plot that has its twists and turns but that is clearly in the writer's mind. We need hardly add that we are *not* saying that when one first sits down to draft an essay, the entire essay is in one's mind. Not at all; throughout *Current Issues* we argue that the act of writing is a way of getting ideas, of (so to speak) finding out what one thinks about a topic. But when one *revises* a draft, one then thinks seriously about how one will present the material effectively to a reader, and one is concerned with opening sentences, transitions, and so forth.

Chiswick's first paragraph ends by more or less setting forth the implications of the opening sentence: If there are jobs that Americans won't do, and if there are no immigrants to do them, will the lettuce go unpicked, lawns unmowed, plates unwashed? The second paragraph bluntly says that "this assertion seems implausible." We have one minor quarrel with the writing here: The first paragraph does *not* end with an "assertion"; rather, it ends with a series of questions. Still, we understand what Chiswick means, and we think his second paragraph is effective. It pretty clearly compels the reader to agree that the position set forth in the first paragraph is "implausible"—of course the lettuce will get picked, the dishes will get washed, and so on. Further, Chiswick offers a statistic that seems compelling; immigrants are concentrated in six states (we probably didn't know this, but it seems plausible; we have no reason to doubt it), and even within these six states, immigrants "are concentrated in a few metropolitan areas." This all makes sense; Chiswick seems to know what he is talking about, and probably readers feel that they can trust him. Additional statistics in the third paragraph help to convey the idea that Chiswick is knowledgeable. We should add, too, that his statistics do not overwhelm the reader. Chiswick does not sandbag us, does not offer so many statistics that we can't follow him or that we decide this sort of thing is not for us. His piece is reader-friendly.

He begins his sixth paragraph with "True," a transition that tells the readers he is conceding something, but that also tells them that the concession does not undermine his thesis. When we teach, we find that we can't overemphasize the importance of transitions, which is partly to say that when we read students' essays, we regularly encounter interesting points but we are not clear where the author is going. When in a conference we point out that words such as *but, on the other hand,* or *further* are missing, students often express surprise.

Chiswick nicely begins his final paragraph with a transition ("The point is"). Also of interest, in terms of his strategies as a writer, is his upbeat ending and his implicit congratulation of the reader, who is presumably an American citizen rather than an undocumented immigrant. Chiswick speaks of "the genius of the American people"—hey, that's you and me—and of their "ingenuity"—that's *our* ingenuity. How can we disagree with a writer who has such a high opinion of us?

John Tierney

Ángels in America (p. 622)

As we see it, Tierney's fundamental argument is an appeal to fairness. Tierney himself comes across as a nice guy (here we are talking about *ethos*), and he presents Ángel as a nice guy (hardworking family man—though, yes, by illegally entering into the United States "he violated the law," as Tierney admits in para. 6). Incidentally,

Ángel's very name helps to establish him as a good guy, but in any case, whatever his name, he seems to be a pillar of society: He began with a low-paying job, worked his way up to better-paying jobs, is married, owns a home, has a daughter, pays taxes, is striving to improve his English. All that can be said against him, apparently, is that he entered our country illegally, and we can hardly blame an impoverished Mexican for trying to improve his life.

Again, Tierney relies chiefly on the issue of fairness: Is it fair that Tierney's grandfather could come here from Ireland and become a citizen, but Ángel, a man whose career resembles that of Tierney's grandfather, cannot? But we should add that Tierney does offer supporting evidence. He gives us details about Ángel's life—his jobs, his income, the cost of his house, the fact that his daughter speaks English, and so on. He also reports some counterarguments, and then he offers counterarguments to those counterarguments. For example, he says that some people say that Mexicans do not assimilate as well as earlier immigrants because Mexicans are closer to home than most earlier immigrants; he then points out that the children of these Mexican immigrants *do* assimilate for example, they speak English (paras. 7–8).

Still, the strength of Tierney's argument is chiefly in its appeal to our sense of fairness and—we think this is important—its appeal to readers who resemble Tierney, that is, whose grandparents or great-grandparents came to this country when it was easy to enter. Of course such a person might say, "Yes, my grandparents just walked in, and I am immensely grateful that they did, but, well, things have changed, and, er, tough. We now have laws, and that's that. My grandparents were lucky, and therefore I was lucky. Guys like Ángel are out of luck. Too bad, I'm sorry, but it's not my fault. The law is the law, and that's that." One might say something along these lines—but one also might *not* say it, might feel that "Yes, America is a place where hardworking folks like my grandparents were welcomed and we should still welcome such people. Further, we should realize that they are an asset to our country."

Question: Does Tierney go too far in the direction of tugging at our heartstrings when he ends his essay by imagining Ángel saying, "I would like them [Republicans on Capitol Hill] to tell my American daughter why her father can't stay with her"? (Our own answer is that Tierney makes a mistake by ending thus. It's a bit too easy to reply, "You want us to tell her why? OK, we will tell her that her father entered illegally.") In our view, he should have quit a bit earlier in the paragraph, when he raised the question of whether Ángel is "less deserving than [the Republicans'] immigrant ancestors."

Victor Davis Hanson

Our Brave New World of Immigration (p. 624)

First, a word about Victor Davis Hanson's title. The words *brave new world* come originally from Shakespeare's *The Tempest* (5.1.183), where the innocent Miranda utters them when she sees the persons who have been shipwrecked on the island where she has lived since infancy, with only her father (Prospero), the spirit Ariel, and the monster Caliban. The entire speech runs this:

> O wonder!
>
> How many goodly creatures are there here!
> How beauteous mankind is! O brave new world,
> That has such people in't.

Brave means something like "splendid," "excellent," a meaning that survives in *bravo*, a shout expressing approval of excellence. Prospero, who has seen much more of life and has firsthand knowledge of the wicked behavior that characterizes much of life—he and Miranda had been ousted from their kingdom by his villainous brother and set adrift in a rotten boat that took them to the island—wryly comments, "'Tis new to thee."

Brave new world thus has from the start, in Shakespeare, an ironic tone: Miranda is *not* speaking ironically—she means what she says—but her father (and the audience) knows that the world is *not* the splendid thing she takes it to be. The phrase is famous because Aldous Huxley used it as the title of a novel, *Brave New World* (1932), a dystopian novel (a book showing an ironic utopia, an imagined world that conceals its horror) in which people are carefree but only because they are drugged and because many of the things that we value, such as art, literature, and religion, have been eliminated from their lives. In short, although Miranda uses the phrase *un*ironically, because Huxley's book is so widely known, the phrase today is almost always ironic, as it is in Hanson's use. For Hanson, an America filled with immigrants is a utopia on the rocks, a society that no right-thinking American wants to see or live in.

The title of the essay immediately engages those readers who have heard the phrase before and who may have read Huxley's novel. The first paragraph expresses sympathy and perhaps even admiration for "Mexican laborers [who] do the backbreaking work of weeding cotton, thinning tree fruit, and picking strawberries." The second paragraph continues to describe crews of workers, but now a faintly ominous note is introduced: These workers "provide the sort of unmatched labor at the sort of wages that their eager employers insist they cannot find among citizens." So, we are told that (1) these workers work very cheaply and that (2) "eager employers insist" Americans won't accept these wages. At least in retrospect, we can hear alarm bells in *eager* and *insist*—a hint that Hanson will take a different view. And indeed, the very next paragraph begins, "But," and by the end of this one-sentence paragraph, we are told that "there is something terribly wrong with a system predicated on a cynical violation of the law."

The next paragraph, the fourth, narrates a story about a dreadful accident in which a van with migrants hit a pickup truck and exploded, killing three people and injuring eight others. Hanson reports his story cautiously ("Perhaps the van had blown a bald tire. Perhaps the driver was intoxicated"), and he explains that "we will probably never know" because "the driver ran away from the carnage of the accident" (para. 5). He does not express outrage that the driver left the scene of the accident; rather, Hanson merely observes, in a factual way, "That often happens when an illegal alien who survives an accident has no insurance or driver's license."

In short, Hanson is establishing a persona (cautious, thoughtful writer, sympathetic to hardworking immigrants, reporting the sad facts), and at the same time he is showing "the carnage" that immigrants—or at least *these* immigrants—in their vans cause. He goes on (para. 7): "Such mayhem is no longer an uncommon occurrence here," and he gives some examples that he has witnessed. Then he gets a bit more specific, mentioning (para. 8) "young males from Mexico," some "60 percent . . . without a high-school degree," who presumably are the causes of this "carnage" (para. 5) and "mayhem" (para. 7). But there is nothing personal, nothing to suggest animosity toward these Mexicans who "send nearly half of their hard-won checks back to kin in Mexico" (para. 8). Still, a reader must begin to wonder: Gee, isn't this a situation that we *must* do something about? How long can we tolerate Mexicans who cause carnage and mayhem?

In his ninth paragraph Hanson recognizes that "many Americans—perhaps out of understandable and well-meant empathy for the dispossessed who toil so hard for so little—support this present open system of non-borders." Hanson *does* see things from another point of view, but he quickly adds, "I find nothing liberal about it," and presumably his readers are ready to agree with him.

From this point onward, Hanson is outspoken in his hostility. In the final third of the essay, he speaks of "zealots," "cynicism" and "a venal Mexican government" (para. 10), and of "a perpetual class of unassimilated recent illegal arrivals" (para. 12). His final two paragraphs are directed not against immigrants, but against those of us—Americans—who do not require immigrants to accept the "bargain of an American melting pot" and who are "happy" enough when the migrants in their vans keep "out of sight and out of mind." But his last sentence brings us back to his opening paragraph: "Sometimes, though, they tragically do not."

Like so many other skillful essayists, Hanson ends by returning to something he set up at the beginning. We have heard some teachers of writing complain that this structure is a cliché, and they caution their students against using it. We differ.

Cardinal Roger Mahony

Called by God to Help (p. 627)

The idea that refusing to aid a fellow human being in need violates a higher law, "the law of God" (question 3), is not a new idea; it is found in the Bible and has been invoked by saints and martyrs ever since. It is the card that trumps all aces. And it is perfectly appropriate for a cardinal to invoke it where he can. Of course it is not a persuasive argument for others, who must rely either on secular reasoning or religious views that are not Judeo-Christian or Muslim. But does a God-fearing cardinal have no other option than disobedience of the sort Mahony favors? We think not.

First (as to question 4), we hear nothing from Mahony about priests being ready to go to jail for their beliefs, as was essential to the classic doctrine of civil disobedience practiced by Henry David Thoreau, Mohandas Gandhi, and Martin Luther King Jr. One might argue that go-to-jail disobedience is implicit in the cardinal's essay. Even so, it's better to make such inferences explicit and not leave them to guesswork.

Second, Mahony does not discuss the practice of past centuries when Catholic priests recused themselves from compliance with Protestant clerical orders. And so he does not discuss whether he should counsel the priests under his authority to recuse themselves from compliance with the demands of the proposed Border Protection, Antiterrorism, and Illegal Immigration Control bill, if it or something like it were to be enacted.

As to question 1, we are not told by the cardinal whether the proposed law imposes mandatory rather than discretionary punishment for violations. If the law imposes mandatory punishment, the case for disobedience is, we think, stronger than if a judge or jury is given discretion as to the sentencing of a convicted offender who violates the law in order to provide humanitarian assistance. Under a discretionary punishment—but not under a mandatory punishment—the sentencer can take into account the intentions of the violator, which, in cases of this sort, are crucial to understanding the behavior of a priest who obeys the cardinal's orders by violating the law.

As to question 5, we think it highly likely that no sensible prosecutor would proceed against a priest who disobeys the law out of respect for his cardinal's orders, especially when the priest can argue that he is facing a moral dilemma: Either way, he acts in violation of the law, the moral law as interpreted by the cardinal and the statutory law as interpreted by the criminal courts. As to exaggerating the threat, the cardinal might well argue that once this law is enacted, it becomes possible—even if it remains unlikely—for the criminal courts to act against the liberty of the priests. How much this exaggerates the plight of the priests is hard to say for certain, as it involves the decisions of many different officials with the power to inflict or withhold punishment.

One way to look at the difference between providing humanitarian assistance without also supporting illegal immigration is to invoke the doctrine of double effect (most familiar to us in the Catholic understanding of abortion and euthanasia). The cardinal might argue that, whereas the provision of humanitarian aid is an intentional act, the support for illegal immigration—admittedly a consequence of the aid—is not the intention of the donor, even though it is a foreseeable result of the aid.

A Note about this selection: As we note in the headnote and in question 8, in January 2013, Cardinal Mahony was relieved of his clerical and administrative duties due to his involvement in attempting to cover up the Church's sexual abuse of boys by priests. We were torn about whether or not to include this essay, which we have included in previous editions, because of the damage this new information has done to Mahony's credibility. Do Mahony's crimes nullify his point of view on topics unrelated to the sexual abuse scandal, or may his ethos be preserved on certain issues though it is thoroughly discolored on others? This is a question you might want to raise among your students, as we do in the questions that follow the essay. In the end, we decided Mahony's point of view still contributed interesting points to a discussion of immigration, but we would have felt remiss if we had not acknowledged his role in covering up unconscionable acts that occurred under the watch of the Archdiocese of Los Angeles.

25
Service: Should the United States Require Young People to Perform Public Service? (p. 630)

Barack Obama

Commencement Address (p. 630)

President Obama offers in his commencement address not an argument but a story—the story of his life and the role in it for public service that connects it to events in the recent past—to the Peace Corps in particular and the contributions made by the 164 Wesleyan graduates. He sketches some of the progressive ideas—expanding the Foreign Service and the Peace Corps—that he intends to implement in his administration. The result is a mixture of stories and events, episodes, and travels that take the listener on a journey of hope and aspiration.

One theme that runs through Obama's remarks is the theme of public service. He mentions several forms such service can take—as it has taken in his life from community service in Chicago to the White House. He does not give an exhaustive list of such kinds of service—that would be tedious and not appropriate for the occasion. Perhaps the most significant form of public service that he doesn't mention is service in the armed forces. Perhaps he doesn't mention it because he never served in the military.

A second theme runs through Obama's address: the life and career of Senator Ted Kennedy, who at the time (May 2008) was terminally ill (Kennedy died in August 2009). Obama uses his sketch of Kennedy's life to make vivid many of the ideas for public service that he wants to illustrate. Not everybody admires and respects the senator. On the contrary, Kennedy embodied all the things that right-wing politicians abhor. But for liberals, Kennedy was the outstanding example of public service in our time. It is therefore appropriate for President Obama to end his address by recounting the many kinds of examples of such service that Senator Kennedy provided.

Peter Levine

The Case for "Service" (p. 636)

As Peter Levine explains in his third paragraph, public service, as he intends to use that term, involves "a variety of programs funded by the government but often organized by private contractors." That is pretty vague—and abstract as well, as Levine (a philosopher) presumably realizes. So he offers us a more detailed conception of public service that remedies these faults (if that is what they are). This more detailed account is embodied in the Kennedy-Hatch Serve America Act of 2008 (S.3487). Indeed, for all practical purposes, the conception of public service that is the focus of Levine's essay is the conception that underlies this act.

Levine specifies (para. 2) three "social objectives" that this act would address by providing subsidies: reducing the dropout rate in schools and colleges, improving public health, and treating energy as a scarce resource. Thus your work as a volunteer for Habitat for Humanity, however admirable it might be, would not count as public service in the sense of this act, because Habitat is funded entirely by volunteer workers and receives no government funding. What about the private contractor Blackwater International, hired in the public sector to carry out American security operations in Iraq and Afghanistan? That organization won't count either, only this time the reason is the military nature of the services it rendered. Levine wants to know in each case whether "an expanded civilian service initiative with these priorities merits government support" (para. 3). His essay has the purpose of explaining and justifying an affirmative answer, and he does so in cautious, measured tones.

One of the vexing problems that faces anyone eager to expand public service into new arenas is whether participation ought to be *mandatory*. Another is whether participation ought to be *universal*. If it's mandatory, there will be decent and law-abiding citizens, like the Amish, who will be inclined not to participate because they refuse to render any kind of government service that is enforced by law. Levine seems not to have any worries along these lines; perhaps they are not deeply troubling because the numbers of such conscientious objectors would be very small (as has proved to be true with the military draft in all of our wars in this century).

The other problem, whether participation ought to be as wide as possible—indeed, universal—is more significant, and Levine recognizes it as such. His remedy? Out of about 14.5 million citizens eighteen or older who are possible enrollees in such programs, space should be provided for 250,000 participants. Anything with much larger enrollment would burden available resources beyond the manageable. Anything with much smaller enrollment would fail to yield a cohort large enough to make a noticeable impact. These seem to us to be reasonable parameters. Even so, the reader cannot fail to note that reasonable as these numbers are, they are based pretty obviously on estimates that are subject to radical revision in light of facts that could be uncovered only by some form of empirical test or trial run (paras. 16–18).

Throughout his essay, Levine shows he is sensitive to the difference between advocating a certain program, say, for employing teenagers in the good-faith belief that if it is adopted it will reduce teenage crime, and the belief that the program as advocated actually achieves measurable success in that endeavor. A useful exercise would be to make a list of a dozen or so of the programs Levine mentions and then to indicate the extent of our knowledge about the success that these programs have so far achieved. The classic example of a case where this distinction was not clearly made is found in the work of Robert Martinson in the early 1970s, when he exposed the failure of programs for penal reform to reach their putative rehabilitative goals.

Levine next turns to the issue of explaining and remedying the "identity gap" between the citizenry and their local, state, and federal governments. That there is such a gap we must grant. The explanation for the gap that Levine favors is professionalization in the form of a "growing monopoly over education by credentialed, professional experts, especially state and district administrators and test-writers" (para. 20). Whether programs of the sorts that Levine deplores should be shelved in favor of programs he could support is largely a political question. Many such programs are known to be available; what is missing is the funding for them. As for the explanation of the gap, there are alternatives to the one Levine favors, such as this one: For some years, even decades, the growth of two-income families has reduced the time and energy available to the parents of school-age children to take an active interest in the education of their children. To be sure, this is only an empirical hypothesis. But it is a perfect case of what Levine himself notes when he says "it is only a hypothesis that community service is an efficient and effective way to address national problems" (para. 8).

At the end of the day you will want to decide whether Levine has shown why he favors creation of programs and policies that reflect the changes he would like to see adopted, and whether he is right to be reasonably optimistic that some, if not all, such changes are feasible.

Thomas E. Ricks

Let's Draft Our Kids (p. 645)

Probably we can separate two large issues: (1) Ought we to have a draft, so that (in General McChrystal's words, quoted in Ricks's first paragraph) the entire nation "has skin in the game" if there is a war? (2) If it is agreed that there should be a draft, is Ricks's proposal, with its three options, a good one? There is plenty here to discuss, and we are confident that students will have plenty to say, even if they do nothing more than respond to the questions that we append to the essay.

Ricks begins his essay in a fairly traditional way, with a quotation from an authority. What makes the quotation of more than routine interest is that—as Ricks explains in his second paragraph—the point of view expressed is *unusual* for a high-ranking officer, and thus the reader is interested to see what Ricks will do with it.

A word about Ricks's final paragraph (in our fifth question we ask students to discuss the writer's strategies here): Ricks published his essay in July 2012, only seven months after the conflict in Iraq had come to an official end (December 18, 2011); so his claim that a draft of the sort he proposes "might . . . make American think more carefully before going to war" would, of course, have had an immediacy that it cannot have today. Still, we think it is a highly effective ending.

Dave Eggers

Serve or Fail (p. 648)

We think there is some confusion over what Dave Eggers wants. His paragraph 12 clearly speaks of "the unwilling college volunteer"—an oxymoron if ever there was one: If the students are unwilling, then they are not volunteers, and if they are volunteers, then they are not unwilling. But in the same paragraph he speaks of the "transformative" powers of volunteering—something that does not happen, he implies, under a coercive practice.

Here's a student exercise suggested by the confusion cited above. Divide up Eggers's essay into three columns under the following headings: (1) passages in which he seems to want volunteers, (2) passages in which he seems to want full student participation, even if coerced, and (3) passages that are ambiguous. As for which position is the dominant one, we leave that to be decided by carrying out the sorting exercise described above. Our hunch is that category (2) will turn out to be dominant.

Part Six

ENDURING QUESTIONS: ESSAYS, A STORY, POEMS, AND A PLAY

26
What Is the Ideal Society? (p. 655)

We at first thought of having a section titled "Utopia," but as we worked on it, the idea seemed needlessly limited, and "Utopia" gave way to the present chapter. Still, several of the readings we give here are utopian. The utopian element in this section allows us here to introduce a comment by Gertrude Himmelfarb, in *Marriage and Morals among the Victorians* (1986):

> "Utopian" is one of the more ambiguous words in our vocabulary. To some it signifies an ideal that is commendable if not entirely realistic, a goal to aspire to, a vision of excellence that leads us, if not to the best, then at least to the better—a benign and altogether innocent image. To others it suggests exactly the opposite, a dangerous illusion which tempts us, in the name of the best, to reject the better and end up with the worse. The yearning for perfection that makes reality seem irredeemably flawed creates so large a discrepancy between the ideal and the reality that nothing less will suffice than a total transformation of reality—of society, the polity, the economy, above all, of human nature.

Thomas More

From *Utopia* (p. 655)

For a sampling of the amazing variety of interpretations of Thomas More's *Utopia*, one has to look at only the essays reprinted in the Norton Critical Edition of *Utopia* (1975), edited by Robert M. Adams. *Utopia* has been seen, for example, as a book advocating Christianity (in particular, Roman Catholicism), communism, or colonialism. It seems fairly clear to us, however, that More is not advocating any of these things, at least not as an end in itself. Rather, in this humanistic work, he is giving his version of an ideal state based on *reason* alone. But he is a Christian speaking to Christians; presumably his sixteenth-century readers were supposed to say to themselves, "If people without revelation can achieve this degree of decency, surely we, with Christ's help, can achieve more. Our society is far inferior to Utopia; let us strive to equal and then to surpass it."

Perhaps the best short essay on *Utopia* is Edward Surtz's introduction to the Yale paper edition, though Father Surtz sees the book as more Christian than do many other commentators. Among Surtz's points are these:

1. The Utopians are typically Renaissance people, balancing Epicureanism with Christianity, having the best of both worlds. They pursue personal pleasure "until it conflicts with social or religious duties, that is, with the just claims of God or fellow citizens" (p. xiv). The term *pleasure* covers many kinds of actions, from scratching an itch to doing virtuous deeds.

2. Utopian communism "is not an end in itself but the best means to the end: pleasure for all the citizens collectively as well as individually" (p. xiv). "The ultimate Utopian ideal of communism is . . . to be of one mind. . . . Sharing material possessions can succeed only if there is first one heart and soul in all" (p. xv).

3. Modern critics too often emphasize More's political, social, and economic innovations and neglect his opinions on education, ethics, philosophy, and religion.

4. More's Utopians are not saints; some are even criminals. More does *not* believe, as some moderns do, that people can be conditioned (brainwashed) to think they are freely cooperating in a society that in fact enslaves them. More's Utopians have some leeway, as in the choice of an occupation and in the use of leisure. Believing in the immutability of the soul, they believe that one's final end is not worship of the state but union with the Absolute.

Most students, when asked for the meaning of *utopian*, will come up with such pejorative words as *unrealistic, impractical, escapist*. They will be surprised, then, to see how realistic More's view of human nature is. He is fully aware, for instance, of such vices as laziness and, especially, pride—not only in nonutopian countries but even in Utopia. Indeed, he seems to feel that most of our ills are due to pride. To restrain pride, almost all Utopians must engage in manual labor and must wear a simple garment, and, again to restrain pride, there is no private property. Notice that More does not put the blame for our wicked actions entirely on private property or on any other economic factors. True, he does say that Europeans greedily seek to attain superfluities because they fear they may some day be in want, but it is evident that even Utopia has wrongdoers. That is, even the utopian system cannot prevent some people from engaging in wicked behavior. More does think, however, that some systems allow our wicked natures to thrive, and so he devises a political, economic, and social system that keeps down pride (the root of the other deadly sins).

But it is not only pride that is kept in check. Utopia is severely regulated in many ways. For instance, Utopians are free to do what they wish during their leisure time—provided that they don't loaf, gamble, or hunt. Similarly, they are free to talk—provided that they don't talk politics, except at special times. Discussion of state affairs, except at the appointed times and places, is punishable by death. George Orwell's Big Brother is present in More's Utopia, but R. W. Chambers is probably right when he argues (in his *Thomas More* [1935]) that Utopia is founded not on terrorism, but on "religious enthusiasm," in particular on faith in God and in the immortality of the soul. Still, even "religious enthusiasm" has, for many readers, something unpleasant about it—something too monastic, too rigid, too disciplined, too cold.

Although one understands and sympathizes with More's condemnation of the pride that engenders social injustice, one can't help but feel that Utopia, with its rational distribution of labor and its evening lectures on edifying topics, is the poorer for lacking the messy vitality of life. (In Utopia, everything seems terribly static: The constitution doesn't change, population is fixed, clothing is uniform, freedom of thought is limited.) On the other hand, we must remember that in the Europe of More's day (and still in much of the world), the masses had to toil from sunrise to sunset to live at a subsistence level. Today's college students (and their professors) find More's Utopia overly restrictive, but they should remember that (1) it is a society of material prosperity for all citizens and a society with a good deal of leisure, and (2) it was freer and more tolerant than any of the European societies of its day.

Additional Topics for Critical Thinking and Writing

1. Can it be said that whatever the merits or weaknesses of More's proposal, he has astutely diagnosed the problems of society?

2. More's spokesman says that European society "is a conspiracy of the rich to advance their own interests under the pretext of organizing society" (para. 41). Can the same be said of our society? Explain.

3. Is More's view of human nature "utopian" in the modern sense of the word; that is, is it uncharacteristically benign? Explain.

Niccolò Machiavelli

From *The Prince* (p. 669)

Harvey Mansfield Jr., in the introduction to his translation of *The Prince* (1985), argues that for Niccolò Machiavelli, the only moral laws are those made by human beings: "The rules or laws that exist are those made by governments or other powers acting under necessity, and they must be obeyed out of the same necessity. Whatever is necessary may be called just or reasonable, but justice is no more reasonable than what a person's prudence tells him he must acquire for himself, or submit to, because men cannot afford justice in any sense that transcends their own preservation" (p. xi).

This reading seems, in a way, much like the work of Karl Marx, who argues that ideology (including ideas of justice) is created by the ruling class, though Marx also seems to believe that because this class achieved power through historical necessity, its ideals—during the period in which it holds power—indeed are true. Witness Marx's praise of the bourgeoisie for redeeming the masses from the "idiocies" of rural life.

Perhaps the heart of the issue is this: Although we may believe that we should be governed by people of honor, Machiavelli (and most utilitarians) would argue that personal goodness and political usefulness are distinct things. A person may be an adulterer, a liar, a sadist, or whatever but may still be an effective guardian of the state. Or, expressed more mildly, a governor may sometimes have to sacrifice personal morality for the safety of the state. Bernard Williams argues, in *Public and Private Morality* (Stuart Hampshire, ed., 1978), that to preserve civilized life, we need politicians who can bring themselves to behave more badly than we ourselves could do. We want them to be as good as possible—and certainly not to be people who act wickedly on a whim or take pleasure in acting wickedly —but to be able to sacrifice personal moral values for political ones. (This idea makes for lively class discussion.)

A related point: If a leader is widely regarded as immoral, he or she loses an important strength: the goodwill of the public. A small example: A senator who is known to have extramarital affairs can probably survive and can be an effective and even an important senator, but a senator who is regarded as a lecher probably cannot.

On the question of whether cruelty may be beneficial to the state: Machiavelli apparently believed that before a state can be justly ruled, there must be a ruler, and to survive, the ruler must be cunning and ruthless. One wonders, of course, if a person with these qualities will also act reasonably, using power for the well-being of the state rather than for purely personal goals. Machiavelli, living in the turmoil of early sixteenth-century Italy, concentrates on the qualities necessary for a leader to survive. Thomas More (see the previous selection in the text), on the other hand, shows us a utopia with almost no political problems, and thus he can concentrate on the morality of the state rather than on the personal characteristics of the governors. Or put it this way: In Machiavelli, it is the ruler against his rivals and his subjects, whereas in More, it is society against the individual's unruly passions.

Additional Topics for Critical Thinking and Writing

1. Imitating Machiavelli's style, notably his use of contrasting historical examples, write an essay of 500 words, presenting an argument on behalf of your own view of some quality necessary in a leader today. You may, for example, want to argue that a leader must be a master of television appearances or must be truthful, compassionate, or versed in history. Your essay will, in a sense, be one chapter in a book called *The Prince Today*.

2. James M. Burns's biography of President Franklin Delano Roosevelt is titled *Roosevelt: The Lion and the Fox* (1956). Judging from your rereading of this selection

from *The Prince*, indicate in a paragraph the characteristics of Roosevelt that the biographer is suggesting by this title. Read Burns's biography and write a thousand-word essay in which you evaluate the aptness of the title, given the facts about Roosevelt's career and Machiavelli's views.

Thomas Jefferson

The Declaration of Independence (p. 678)

In discussing almost any argument (for that matter, in discussing any writing), it is usually helpful to consider the intended or imagined *audience(s)*. With minimal assistance, students can see that the Declaration of Independence has several audiences (question 1). These audiences can perhaps be described thus:

1. The "candid world" (para. 5), addressed out of "a decent respect to the opinions of mankind" (para. 1)

2. The king and his ministers (the grievances are blamed on them)

3. The British people (students who do a research paper on the Declaration will learn that some passages censuring the British people were deleted to maintain good relations)

4. France (the Declaration announces that the "United Colonies" have "full power to levy War, conclude Peace, contract Alliances, establish Commerce, and to do all other Acts and Things which Independent States may of right do." Most historians see in these words a bid for foreign aid—military supplies from France)

5. Those colonists who were not eager for independence

Attention may be given to the *speaker* of the Declaration—that is, to the self-image (question 3) that the colonists present. Jefferson refers to "a decent respect to the opinions of mankind" (para. 1), and he admits that "Governments long established should not be changed for light and transient causes" (para. 4). Notice, too, his assertion that "We Have Petitioned for Redress in the most humble terms" (para. 33). In short, the colonists present themselves not as radicals or firebrands, but as patient, long-suffering people who are willing to put their case before the tribunal of the world. Notice such words as *duty, necessary*, and *necessity*. They are not rebels; rather, they have been "plundered" and "ravaged" and are exerting a right—the right of the people to alter or to abolish a government that fails to fulfill the legitimate purpose of government (para. 4).

Some attention in class can also be profitably given to discussing the *structure* of the work:

1. The first sentence announces the colonists' purpose, explaining "the causes which impel them to the separation."

2. The core of the document is an exposition of the causes, in two sections:

   a. Theoretical and general justification (for example, "self-evident" truths) and

   b. The list of despotic British actions.

3. The Declaration concludes with the response of the colonies (the signers pledge their lives).

Students can also be shown how the explicit assumptions of the Declaration—

1. All men are created equal and are endowed with "unalienable rights,"

2. Governments are instituted to preserve these rights,

3. People have a duty and a right to throw off a despotic government,

— can be cast into this *syllogism:*

1. If a government is despotic, the people have a right to overthrow it and to form a new government.

2. The British government of the American colonies is despotic.

3. Therefore, the people have a right to overthrow it and to form a new government.

The major premise is not argued but is asserted as an "unalienable right." The minor premise is arrived at inductively (instances are cited, and a generalization is drawn from them).

Additional Topics for Critical Thinking and Writing

1. The Declaration is an argument for revolution in a particular society. Investigate conditions in some society (for example, Cuba, China, Iran, El Salvador, Nicaragua), and argue that, on the grounds of the Declaration, people in that society do—or do not—have the right to revolt.

2. Read Chapter 19 of John Locke's *Essay Concerning Civil Government* (first published in 1690) and write a 500-word essay in which you identify all those passages or ideas found in Locke that appear also in the Declaration. Are there any ideas in Locke's chapter that have no parallel in the Declaration but that nevertheless seem to you to be relevant to its purpose and content?

Elizabeth Cady Stanton

Declaration of Sentiments and Resolutions (p. 682)

Elizabeth Cady Stanton's Declaration of 1848 is the historic precursor of the decade-long effort that finally failed in 1982 to enact an Equal Rights Amendment (ERA) to the Constitution. The Fourteenth Amendment, enacted twenty years after the first Woman's Rights Convention at Seneca Falls, New York, did provide that no state "shall . . . deprive any person of life, liberty, or property without due process of law, nor deny any person within its jurisdiction the equal protection of the laws." At face value, that might look like the rejection of gender as a basis for lawful discrimination. Opponents of ERA in the 1970s who professed sympathy with feminist claims for constitutional equality often pointed to the language quoted as if that settled the matter. Not so, however.

The term *male* entered the Constitution in the Fourteenth Amendment itself (see section 2), thereby helping to etch more clearly the implicit and historic male bias of the Constitution and the laws from the beginning and indicating that "due process" and "equal protection" were not to be given a gender-free reading. An Illinois case of 1873 settled this issue for decades. Arguing that she was entitled under the Fourteenth Amendment to be admitted to the bar, Myra Bradwell unsuccessfully fought her case through the state courts to the U.S. Supreme Court. The language of the majority's decision enshrined in constitutional interpretation the worst excesses of male chauvinism (see *Bradwell v. Illinois*, 83 U.S. 130 [1873]). Even the right to vote ("elective franchise") (para. 4) was not incorporated into the Constitution until 1920 (the Nineteenth Amendment). Full equality of the sexes under the laws and the Constitution, whether or not it is a good thing, still does not exist in our society.

Civil death (question 3) is the ultimate extreme to which a person can be reduced: denial by law of all civil rights, privileges, immunities, and liberties. (Not even prisoners on death row, today, suffer civil death.) Stanton elaborates the point (paras. 9–11). It was commonplace among feminists of the nineteenth century to point out that marriage under law was functionally equivalent to civil death.

107

It was not, however, functionally equivalent to chattel slavery (which was to last another fifteen years after the Seneca Falls Convention; not surprisingly, the women who organized the convention were staunch abolitionists). It might be a useful classroom exercise for students to explore the differences under law in the 1840s between the status of American white women, as the Declaration reports it, and the status of American black slaves. An excellent source for slave law is A. Leon Higginbotham Jr., *In the Matter of Color* (1978).

Martin Luther King Jr.

I Have a Dream (p. 687)

The setting (the steps of the Lincoln Memorial, in Washington, D.C., on the centennial of the Emancipation Proclamation) plays an important part in this speech. By the way, few students know that the Emancipation Proclamation did not in fact free any slaves. In 1862, President Lincoln announced that he would declare free the slaves of any state that did not return to the Union. None of the states that had seceded accepted the invitation to return, and so on January 1, 1863, he announced the Emancipation Proclamation. It did not apply to slaves in states such as Maryland and Kentucky that had chosen to stay in the Union, and of course, it had no force in the Confederacy. Still, the symbolic importance of the Proclamation was and is immense, and it is part of King's speech.

King's association with Lincoln is evident not only in the setting but also in the language. The opening words, "Five score," evoke the "Four score and seven years ago" of the Gettysburg Address, and Lincoln himself was evoking the language of the Bible. King's speech, too, richly evokes the Bible ("dark and desolate valley," "God's children," "cup of bitterness," "trials and tribulations," "storms of persecution," "every hill and mountain shall be made low, the rough places will be made plain and the crooked places will be made straight, and the glory of the Lord shall be revealed, and all flesh shall see it together"—this last from Isaiah 40:4–5).

Another symbol, in addition to Lincoln and to the Bible, is the "American dream" (para. 11, but foreshadowed in the title of the speech), which King, like most other Americans, identifies with the remark in the Declaration of Independence that "All men are created equal." King also identifies his dream (and himself) with "My country, 'tis of thee," and (in the final paragraph) with black spirituals.

The exalted language of the Bible and the Declaration is joined with the humble language of commerce, the "promissory note," the "bad check" of paragraphs 3 and 4, and the whole (because it is a speech) is rich in evocative repetition, especially parallelisms (again a biblical device).

All these devices and allusions are fairly obvious, and that is part of their point. King is emphasizing that speaker and audience share a culture; and though the immediate audience in Washington was predominantly black, King knew that his words would also reach a larger audience of whites—whites who share this culture.

The structure (question 6) is this: The first part gives a historical perspective; the second, an exhortation not to fall into evil; the third, an exposition of the dream, a picture of the better world that the hearers can help to bring about.

Additional Topic for Critical Thinking and Writing

King's speech stresses the twin themes of equality and freedom and does not suggest that the two might be in tension or conflict with each other. Do you agree that there is no tension? Try to state precisely the freedom(s) and equalities for which King pleads. Is our society any closer to achieving these goals today, do you think, than in 1963?

W. H. Auden

The Unknown Citizen (p. 691)

In "The Unknown Citizen," the speaker's voice is obviously not the poet's. The speaker—appropriately unidentified in a poem about a society without individuals—is apparently a bureaucrat. For such a person, a "saint" is not one who is committed to spiritual values but one who causes no trouble.

Additional Topics for Critical Thinking and Writing

1. What is W. H. Auden satirizing in "The Unknown Citizen"? (Students might be cautioned to spend some time thinking about whether Auden is satirizing the speaker, the citizen, conformism, totalitarianism, technology, or what.)

2. Write a prose eulogy of 250 words satirizing contemporary conformity or, if you prefer, contemporary individualism.

3. Was the speaker free? Was he happy? Argue your view.

4. In a paragraph or two, sketch the values of the speaker of the poem, and then sum them up in a sentence or two. Finally, in as much space as you feel you need, judge these values.

Langston Hughes

Let America Be America Again (p. 692)

It is sometimes difficult to remember that poets (or at least some of them) once were regarded as national bards, celebrating the ideals of society. On the whole, today we distrust public oratory, and we are much more comfortable with the idea of the poet as the reporter of private feelings. In short, we prefer the private lyric to such public lyric forms as the ode and the hymn. People who believe that poetry ought to address public themes are likely to complain that poetry has turned inward on itself and has retreated from life. They may point out that although there are all sorts of poetry festivals and public readings, the poetry is likely to be confessional—for instance, the expression of the emotions of an abandoned woman, a gay man, or the child of immigrant Jews or Hispanics. In fact, such poems are deeply rooted in the politics and social practices of our age. (For an example, see Mitsuye Yamada, "To the Lady," p. 771.)

Still, it must be said that poems explicitly about the nation—patriotic poems—are now rare. We can hardly imagine a poet today writing something like "Barbara Frietchie" (the stuff of our school days), "Paul Revere's Ride," or "O Captain, My Captain." Today we seem chiefly to value what Harold Bloom has crankily called "The Poetry of Resentment." Hughes did not by any means write the sort of poetry that Bloom castigates, but the Hughes poems that we value most highly do seem to come directly from the life that he observed closely—for instance, his poems about prostitution and poverty in Harlem. But there is another Hughes, the Hughes who for a while saw himself as an heir to Walt Whitman and especially to Carl Sandburg, and it was in this role that he wrote "Let America Be America Again." Although the influence of Whitman and Sandburg was great, Hughes of course drew also on black sources. In particular, the motif that America has been America (the land of the free) only for some whites was common in black prose, for instance, in the writings of Frederick Douglass. Hughes also drew, very evidently, on radical socialist thought, and doubtless that is why (as we indicate in question 3) *Esquire* published only the first fifty lines. Lines 1–50 offer a strong indictment, but they stop short of preaching revolution. The gist of the idea in these lines is that America today should be true to its original ideals, the ideals of the founding fathers. No one can disapprove of this ideal. But Hughes goes a bit further: Blacks, he says, have not shared in this society ("America never was America to me"), and early in the poem, he links the marginalization of blacks with that of poor whites (line 19) and immigrants (line 45). True enough; almost everyone would grant, "Yes, it's not just that today we have lost some of our ideals; we failed from the start to extend them to all of our people." But beyond line 50 the poem gets more radical, as Hughes specifies additional victims—unemployed people on relief (line 53) and Native Americans (line 65). The suggestion that injustice extended to groups beyond blacks must have sounded menacing enough even to the liberal editors of *Esquire*, but in line 73 we hear (and the editors of *Esquire* must have heard) a still more radical note, a call to revolution: "We must take back our land again" and "We, the people, must redeem / The land, the mines, the plants, the rivers" (lines 82–83). The editors doubtless knew that this talk of the redemptive power of "the people," especially as opposed to the "leeches" of line 72, was the voice of the extreme left wing. Our own view, for what it is worth, is that the shorter poem (lines 1–50, as opposed to 1–86) is the better poem, partly, we confess, because the call to "take back" the land is left unexplained.

Ursula K. Le Guin

The Ones Who Walk Away from Omelas (p. 695)

When Thomas More called his book *Utopia*, he punned on the Greek "good place" (*eu topos*) and on "no place" (*ou topos*). Like all of the rest of us, he knew that the fully happy society is "no place," if only because accidents, disease, and death are part of life. Ursula K. Le Guin's narrator gives us a fairly detailed description of an imagined happy society (para. 1)— Omelas is "bright-towered by the sea," the old celebrants in the festival wear "long stiff robes of mauve and gray," and the boys and girls are "naked in the bright air, with mudstained feet and ankles and long, lithe arms"—but the narrator also is vague about many things that we would dearly like to know. For instance, although the narrator tells us that there is no king and there are no slaves in Omelas, the narrator also makes a confession, "I do not know the rules and laws of their society" (para. 3). The story includes other confessions of ignorance, and at one point, the narrator, aware that the narrative thus far has been unconvincing and fairy-tale-like (for example, those bright towers by the sea), almost gives up and urges the reader to imagine Omelas "as your own fancy bids."

Doubtless Le Guin is vague about important matters because she—like everyone else—cannot depict a convincing utopia that can withstand scrutiny. But she is also vague for a more important reason: She is not earnestly writing a utopian tale like, say, Edward Bellamy's *Looking Backward*. Rather, she is raising a moral problem, or, more exactly, she is amplifying a problem that William James had raised. Omelas need not be a convincing presentation of the perfectly happy life, and indeed the narrator makes Omelas most convincing when he (or she?) prefaces the information about the suffering child with these words: "Do you believe? Do you accept the festival, the city, the joy? No? Then let me describe one more thing" (para. 6). When we learn about the wretched child, Omelas becomes much more believable, for we are all aware that much of our happiness in fact depends on the suffering of others. These others may be the exploited workers whose painful labor allows us to eat and dress well; they may be the sick, whose ills make some physicians prosperous; they may be the aggrieved, whose lawsuits pay the college tuition for the children of lawyers; they may even be the suffering animals whose pain in medical laboratories may help to alleviate our own pain. In short, whoever we are, some of our happiness depends on the misfortunes of other creatures—and at times we are aware of this fact. Le Guin's happy city now becomes easily understandable: It is an image not of an ideal world but of our world.

Where a parable usually evokes a fairly clear moral and leaves us in little doubt about how we ought to act, this story leaves us puzzled. It heightens our awareness of a cruel fact of society, but it does not tell us how we can reform our society. Put another way, where does one go when one walks away from Omelas? Can we really envisage the possibility of a happy life that is not in any way based on suffering and injustice somewhere? Is the story therefore pointless, mere fantasy, mere escapism? Presumably, Le Guin is simply seeking to make us think so that we will learn to act in ways that minimize the suffering of others. It is inconceivable that life will ever be utopian, but it is not inconceivable that injustice and human suffering may be reduced.

Additional Topics for Critical Thinking and Writing

1. How convincing does the narrator think the picture of Omelas is? Why do you suppose that Le Guin does not offer details about the laws of the land? Does Omelas become more convincing when we learn about the child? Support your response with evidence.

2. What is the point of walking away from Omelas? Can the walker go to a better society? If not, is the story pointless? (Put another way, the story is a fantasy, but is it also escapist fiction?)

Helen Prejean

Executions Are Too Costly—Morally (p. 701)

Sister Helen Prejean has proved to be the most influential figure—speaker, lobbyist, film consultant, writer, and spiritual adviser to men on death row—currently opposing the death penalty in the United States. Her humor, warmth, and compassion have been much admired, and she has earned the respect of many whose lives have been ravaged by the murder of a loved one—whether in a crime of homicide or in a legally authorized execution. She has brought to the public debate a down-home human approach noticeably absent from much of the discourse on this subject.

The excerpt we reprint from her popular book *Dead Man Walking* is devoted largely to examining the biblical support for (or opposition to) capital punishment. She neglects to mention what many think is the best single passage in the Bible on this subject, Genesis 4:9–16—God's response to Cain for murdering his brother, Abel. God punishes Cain in three ways: He is exiled, he is cursed, and he is stigmatized (so that others will recognize him for the murderer he is). Perhaps no other passage in the Bible so personalizes God's punishment meted out to a murderer — not perhaps a perfect paradigm for how today's opponents of the death penalty would have murderers punished, but worthy of their thoughtful reflection.

The Judeo-Christian posture on the death penalty is a long story. A small fraction of it is related in paragraphs 11 through 15. Those who seek more must consult the hefty recent monograph by James J. Megivern, *The Death Penalty: An Historical and Theological Survey* (1997). Professor Megivern explains how the Christian church at the time of the First Crusade (1095) abandoned its early commitment to pacifism in favor of Christian triumphalism with sword in hand, led by Pope Gregory VII (1073–1085), his successor Pope Urban II (1042–1099), and St. Bernard of Clairvaux (1090–1153). Their enemies were infidels (read Jews and Muslims) and soon thereafter Christian heretics. According to Megivern, the epitome of this transformation in the Christian ethic of war and peace, of violence and pacifism, appears in the *Chanson d'Antioche*, "the greatest of the vernacular epics of the First Crusade." Christ is portrayed as hanging on the cross and assuring the good thief to his side that "from over the seas will come a new race which will take *revenge* on the death of the father." Thus, as Megivern notes, was brought to pass a "total reversal of the actual teachings of Jesus."

111

27
How Free Is the Will of the Individual within Society? (p. 706)

Plato

Crito (p. 708)

The headnote in the text gives a fairly full account of the context of *Crito*, both in Socrates' life and in Plato's dialogues. After decades of relative neglect, this dialogue, with its argument over the citizen's obligation to the state, has recently aroused interest among scholars, and several good books (among them those by A. D. Woozley and Richard Kraut) now are available to guide the interested reader through the intricacies of Plato's text.

The dialogue can be divided into three parts of unequal length and importance. In the brief first part (which ends when Crito says "Your death means a double calamity for me," para. 26), Plato does little more than set the stage. In the longer second part (which ends when Socrates offers the plea of "the Laws and Constitution of Athens," para. 91), Crito makes his feeble attempt to persuade Socrates to escape, and Socrates in rather leisurely fashion examines and rejects Crito's reasons. The final and longest part is also the most important because in it, Socrates advances an early version of the social contract argument for political obligation, later made famous and influential by John Locke and Jean-Jacques Rousseau and revived in recent years in the sophisticated moral philosophy of John Rawls (see his *A Theory of Justice*, 1971). Socrates makes no attempt to rebut this long argument; the reader (along with Crito) is led to think that Socrates must, in all honesty, concede each step and so draw the conclusion the Laws want him to draw.

As for the adequacy of this argument (question 6), the notion of a "just agreement" between the individual citizen and the abstract state looks quite implausible if taken literally, even in the city-state of Athens. But if taken as a metaphor or as a model of an ideal relationship between the individual and the laws, then one has to answer this question: How can a hypothetical or ideal relation impose any actual or real obligation on anyone? The result is a classic dilemma for social-contract theorists, not easily resolved.

The dialogue can be effectively paired with Martin Luther King Jr.'s "Letter from Birmingham Jail" (p. 738). The most obvious difference between the positions of Socrates and King (questions 8 and 9) is that Socrates implies that the laws of Athens are just—though, unfortunately, wrongly applied to Socrates himself by his Athenian judges—whereas King asserts that the laws of Alabama are unjust and implies their application to him is unjust. In particular, Socrates implies that he gave his free and informed consent to the authority of the laws of Athens, whereas King implies that black Americans never gave their free consent to segregation laws.

George Orwell

Shooting an Elephant (p. 721)

George Orwell explicitly tells us that his experience as a police officer in Burma was "perplexing and upsetting" (para. 2). (One might compare this statement with the feelings of Thomas Hardy's soldier in "The Man He Killed," p. 755.) He characterizes himself as "young and ill-educated" at the time (clearly in the past), and he says he was caught between his hatred of imperialism and his rage against the Burmese. The essay's paradoxical opening sentence foreshadows its chief point (that imperialism destroys the freedom of both the oppressor and the oppressed), but Orwell devotes the rest of the first paragraph, with its ugly characterizations of the Burmese, to dramatizing his rage. Students unaware of Orwell's preoccupation with decency may fail to understand that the first two paragraphs do not contradict, but reinforce, each other. The racial slurs in the first paragraph and elsewhere in the essay are deliberate; they show the alienation from normal feelings, the violations of self that were, as Orwell goes on to show, the by-products of his role.

That he was playing a role—but a role that captured the player—is highlighted by the theatrical metaphors that accumulate as he is about to shoot the elephant: He sees himself as a "conjurer" with a "magical rifle," as an "actor," and as "an absurd puppet" (para. 7).

The essay's final paragraph, with its cold tone, its conflicting half-truths and rationalizations, again effectively dramatizes the deadening of feeling and loss of integrity that Orwell experienced and that he believes all who turn tyrant experience.

Walter T. Stace

Is Determinism Inconsistent with Free Will? (p. 728)

The general position taken by Walter T. Stace on the free-will controversy is owed—though Stace doesn't mention it—to the Scots philosopher David Hume. In his *Enquiry Concerning Human Understanding* (1748), Section VIII, "Of Liberty and Necessity," Hume argues that if acting of one's own free will means acting without external coercion or internal compulsion, and if "necessity" (or determinism) means that every event has a cause, then there is no incompatibility between the two. We reprint Stace's version of the solution to the free-will problem (a version of what is now called *compatibilism*) rather than Hume's because it is briefer and much more accessible to the modern reader.

The answer to question 1, stated as a formal deductive argument, goes like this:

1. If one acts without free will, then one cannot be held responsible for what one does.

2. If one cannot be held responsible for one's acts, then moral praise and blame—morality, in short—are impossible.

3. Therefore, if one acts without free will, then morality is impossible.

The argument as stated is surely valid. It has the form: If p, then q; if q, then r; therefore, if p, then r—a case of a hypothetical syllogism and a valid form of reasoning. Most philosophers think it is sound; whether it is, of course, depends on the truth of both premises. Of the two, premise 1 is likely to be the more controversial.

Now consider question 9. Here is a valid argument in the spirit of Stace's views in paragraph 28:

1. A person's acts must be the effects of her beliefs and decisions for her to be morally responsible for those acts.

2. A person's acts must be predetermined for those acts to be the effects of her beliefs and decisions.

3. Therefore, unless determinism is true at least as regards a person's acts, no one is morally responsible for anything.

Here, the more problematic premise is the second one.

113

Regarding question 2, a classic example of a purely verbal dispute is arguing whether a glass of water is half full or half empty or whether you are taller than I am or I am shorter than you are. Such disputes are absurd, since in truth, neither party can be correct unless the other is also; what is at stake in the dispute is nothing but each disputant's preferred way of stating the facts. There is no dispute about any fact of the matter.

Stace's claim that the free-will controversy is "merely verbal" or is "a semantic problem" (para. 3) is slightly more complicated. The problem arises because the term *free will* has been incorrectly defined ("by learned men, especially philosophers," he says), with the result that nothing counts as action of one's own free will. This, Stace argues, is absurd because in the ordinary sense of the phrase "He did so-and-so of his own free will," it is perfectly clear that such an imputation has plenty of applications. So Stace in effect says the free-will controversy is "merely verbal" because whether we act with a free will turns entirely on how we define *free will.*

As a side note, Stace's strategy in this essay is reminiscent of the linguistic analytic philosophy that flourished in the 1950s and 1960s here and in Great Britain (though a reader of the book from which our excerpt is taken will find no other evidence of sympathy with that style of philosophy). He proposes to defend the compatibility of free will and determinism by relying on "common usage . . . in ordinary conversation" (para. 6) — that is, he will rely on the way ordinary people talk in deciding whether someone did or did not act of his or her own free will. We think his examples of conversation (paras. 9–10, 14) do reflect ordinary usage and show us how we do use the term *free will.* These snippets also show that people believe they can tell whether someone is acting out of a free will; Stace implies this is enough to show they are correct in this belief (and he does not seem to worry about addressing that issue directly).

Not one to have been overawed by professional academic philosophers — prior to a midcareer move into teaching and writing philosophy, Stace had rendered long years in the British foreign service and, like many of his British academic contemporaries in the early twentieth century, never pursued any postgraduate degrees in philosophy — Stace concocts an outrageous imaginary conversation between a philosopher and a jury foreman (para. 12). The philosopher's unforgivable error, Stace claims, is to think that a person can act of his or her own free will if and only if that act is *not* the effect of any causes. But as the earlier hypothetical dialogues showed, not being the effect of any cause has nothing to do with the meaning of *free will* in ordinary discourse.

Stace does not point out that his pompous philosopher talks as if he had made a momentous discovery: "There is no such thing as free will." Compare that to "there is no such thing as a square circle" and "there is no such thing as a unicorn." Both these propositions are true, but only the latter is true as a matter of fact; the former is true by implicit definition of the terms. Has the philosopher who insists there is no such thing as free will made a discovery about any matter of fact? No. Has he drawn a necessary conclusion from the ordinary meaning of the terms being used? Again, no. (By the way, just what real, as opposed to imaginary, philosophers Stace may have in mind here is not clear to us. His discussion is none the worse if in fact no philosophers ever actually argued as in his example.) So the philosopher's rejection of the very possibility of anyone acting of free will can be entirely ignored.

The classic objection to compatibilism of the sort Stace defends is that it fails to guarantee that there are free *acts* because it fails to guarantee that these acts are the effects of a free *will.* The careful reader will note that the explicit definitions that Stace gives (para. 18) of free versus unfree *acts* are silent on the freedom or unfreedom of the *will.* Libertarians (in the metaphysical, not the political, sense of that term) argue, plausibly enough, that unless the will is free, the acts caused by that will cannot be free. And so one might well reject Stace's definition of "acts done freely" as acts where the "immediate causes are psychological states of the agent" because that is far too broad and too silent on the status of the agent's will. It is too broad because it all depends on just what kind of "psychological state" is in question. For surely a person who acts out of inner

114

compulsion, posthypnotic trance, or an addiction would not be said to act freely. It is too silent because we need to know more about what constitutes the psychological states that do result in free acts. We do not have an adequate theory of free will until we have solved these problems.

For further reading in the spirit of the Hume-Stace approach to the problem of free will, we select from a whole library of books one that is unusually original, informative, and even entertaining, the volume titled *Elbow Room* (1984) by our colleague D. C. Dennett.

Martin Luther King Jr.

Letter from Birmingham Jail (p. 738)

Martin Luther King Jr.'s letter was prompted by a letter (printed in the text) by eight Birmingham clergymen. His letter is unusually long ("Never before have I written so long a letter," para. 48) because he was jailed at the time and thus was unable to speak to audiences face-to-face.

King here goes to some length to show that his work is thoroughly in the American (and Judeo-Christian) tradition. That is, although he rebuts the letter of the eight clergymen, he represents himself not as a radical or in any way un-American (and of course not as an opponent of the Judeo-Christian tradition), but as one who shares the culture of his audience. Thus, although he rejects the clergymen's view that he is impatient, he begins by acknowledging their decency. They are, he says, "men of genuine good will"—and in saying this, King thereby implies that he, too, is a man of good will. Moreover, King's real audience is not only the eight clergymen, but all readers of his letter, who are assumed to be decent folk. Notice, too, in his insistence that he is speaking on an issue that involves all Americans, his statement that "injustice anywhere is a threat to justice everywhere" (para. 4). But his chief strategy early in the letter is to identify himself with Paul (para. 3) and thus to guide his mainly Christian audience to see him as carrying on a tradition that they cherish. Notice also the references to Niebuhr, Buber (a Jew), and Jesus.

It is usual, and correct, to say that King is a master of the appeal to emotion. This essay reveals such mastery, as when he quotes a five-year-old boy: "Daddy, why do white people treat colored people so mean?" (para. 14). And because King is really addressing not so much the eight clergymen as a sympathetic audience that probably needs encouragement to persist rather than reasons to change their beliefs, an emotional (inspirational) appeal is appropriate. But the essay is also rich in lucid exposition and careful analysis, as in paragraph 6 (on the four steps of a nonviolent campaign) and paragraphs 15 and 16 (comparing just and unjust laws).

Additional Topics for Critical Thinking and Writing

1. Think of some injustice that you know something about, and jot down the facts as objectively as possible. Arrange them so that they form an outline. Then, using these facts as a framework, write an essay (possibly in the form of a letter to a specific audience) of about five hundred words, presenting your case in a manner somewhat analogous to King's. For example, don't hesitate to make comparisons with biblical, literary, or recent historical material, to use personal experiences, or to use any other persuasive devices you wish, including appeals to the emotions. Hand in the objective list along with the essay.

2. If some example of nonviolent direct action has recently been in the news, such as actions by persons fearful of nuclear power plants, write an essay evaluating the tactics and their effectiveness in dealing with the issue.

3. Read Plato's *Crito*, and also Plato's *Apology* (in your library). Write an essay of five hundred words explaining whether, as King says, "Socrates practiced civil disobedience (para. 10)."

Peter Cave

Man or Sheep? (p. 752)

Cave opens his essay on a light note, or at least on a lighter note than if he hadn't ended his first paragraph with the final two words ("and long"). As things stand, it is difficult to find much to cheer us up in Hobbes's view of the world, a view that has had few dissenters since 1651, when his great book, *Leviathan*, was published. For it is the main feature of that book—and the social contract theory that it explains and defends—that Cave is leaning on throughout this chapter of his book.

Social contract theory—whose leading historical advocates are Hobbes, John Locke, Jean-Jacques Rousseau, Immanuel Kant, and, in our day, John Rawls—and the theory of political obligation it advocates have the greatest challenge from the moral point of view in confronting the questions: Do we have an obligation to obey the law? Are we obligated by the deeds of our predecessors? Social contract theorists give an affirmative answer to both questions. But are they the correct answers? It is easy to see examples where it appears that they are. Institutions of every variety, shape, and scope are already fully functioning when we arrive at birth. We neither create nor sustain them. But we do benefit from them with or without any desire to do so.

The social contract theory gets its name from the way in which society is thought to be held together by a contract. The contract's central feature is that we are bound by tacit and hypothetical consent (as Cave explains) to create and obey the law, not just because it is advantageous to do so (which it is), but because we owe it to each other to comply with the law and the legal and social institutions that constitute it. It is also easy to see ways in which such a contract is at best a model for rational social relationships rather than anything more descriptive. Surely we are not in fact related to each other by means of a free, voluntary agreement to obey all the laws of our society.

Thomas Hardy

The Man He Killed (p. 755)

Almost every student will be able to report the occurrence of some action they took that seems just to have happened, unwilled and inexplicable. Or if they can explain it, the consequences nevertheless seem vastly disproportionate to the action. With such happenings in mind, one finds oneself murmuring that chance governs all or, if one is given to proverbs, "Man proposes, God disposes." Taking a long view of things, they may comment on how little each of us can actually control by our wills. After all, we did not will our own existence or the family that surrounds us, and it takes only a little thought to realize that, had a different person in the admissions office read our application, we might not have been admitted to the college where we now are taking classes and making friends. And yet most students will also report that they certainly *feel* free—that they can decide to come to class or to cut class, to take this course or that course, to major in this subject or that subject, and to enter this field or that field. Samuel Johnson, in a passage that we reprint in the text, sums up this contradictory state: "All theory is against the freedom of the will; all experience for it."

Thomas Hardy's speaker, presumably a fairly simple, ordinary fellow (notice the diction, which includes such words as "'list" [for "enlist"] and "off-hand-like") who enlisted because he was out of work and had no money, found himself (given the date, probably in

116

South Africa, during the Boer War) face-to-face with another man, who was, he had been told, his "foe," so he did what he was supposed to do: He shot his "foe." The experience has stayed in his mind, and the best *reason* he can offer for his action is to say that war is "quaint and curious." But the fact that he is repeating the story indicates that he himself is not fully satisfied with his own explanation. Presumably he thinks he acted freely, but he is somewhat puzzled by his action. We, with our superior view, can see that he was the victim of economic circumstances (he was unemployed) and the victim of an imperialistic government that used him for its own purposes.

In discussing the poem one may find oneself talking about the irony of fate, whereby a man who joined the army to keep himself alive finds that he has to kill another man who is pretty much like him. Almost surely, students will see that there is a gap between their awareness and the speaker's unawareness, but they may also agree that all of us, no matter how clever we think we are, move in a world that is largely mysterious to us, a world that (in Hamlet's words) "shapes our ends, / Rough-hew them how we will."

T. S. Eliot

The Love Song of J. Alfred Prufrock (p. 756)

Few instructors in introductory courses will encounter students who have much familiarity with poetry, but you may find that some students have read Robert Browning's "My Last Duchess" and have been instructed in the ways of the dramatic monologue, usually defined as a poem with a speaker and a listener. It will be necessary to explain to these students that "Prufrock" is a different sort of monologue, an internal monologue. At least this is the way we take it; the "you" is the speaker's amorous self, addressed by his timorous self. In our view, the speaker does not actually make a visit—or at least may not—and does not speak aloud to anyone; rather, he imagines a visit, with all of its distressing episodes, and we hear an unspoken inner debate. In the words that John Stuart Mill used to characterize lyric poetry, we get "feeling confessing itself to itself."

"Prufrock" gives us a particularly inhibited protagonist, but we assume that all readers can empathize with his sense of paralysis. After all, the epigraph that opens the poem—in medieval Italian, a language that most of us do not know—is in itself almost enough to terrify the reader, to turn all of us into Prufrocks who dare not read another line lest we again reveal our inadequacies. Having said this, we want to assure instructors that the poem *can* be taught effectively, despite all of the footnotes. Students enjoy talking about the speaker's name (a combination of *prude* and *frock*, therefore suggesting what in politically incorrect days was called an *old maid*?), about the people at the cocktail party commenting on Michelangelo, about the comic rhyme of *crisis* and *ices*, about Prufrock momentarily gaining strength by the absurd expedient of thinking about his collar and his stickpin, and so forth. A good way to proceed is to ask a student to read the first stanza and then to invite comments on what the students like (or find especially interesting) about the passage. In our experience, with only a little assistance, they will comment on particularly memorable phrases and images. And so on, stanza by stanza; they may admit, for instance, that Prufrock's terrors (his fear that people will say, "How his arms and legs are thin") are not foreign to their own thoughts. Have they ever feared they would be judged absurd? (We have never gone so far as to ask if they have ever judged themselves absurd.) Do they dare to wear clothing not sanctioned by contemporary fashion?

Susan Glaspell

Trifles (p. 761)

Some students may know Susan Glaspell's other version of this work, a short story titled "A Jury of Her Peers." Class discussion can focus on the interchangeability of the titles.

Trifles could have been called "A Jury of Her Peers," and vice versa. A peer, of course, is an equal, and the suggestion of the story's title is that Mrs. Wright is judged by a jury of her equals—Mrs. Hale and Mrs. Peters. A male jury would not consist of her equals because, at least in the context of the story and the play, males simply don't have the experiences of women and therefore can't judge them fairly.

Murder is the stuff of TV dramas, and this play concerns a murder, of course, but it's worth asking students how the play differs from a whodunnit. Discussion will soon establish that we learn, early in *Trifles,* who performed the murder, and we even know, fairly early, *why* Minnie killed her husband. (The women know what is what because they correctly interpret "trifles," but the men are baffled, since they are looking for obvious signs of anger.) Once we know who performed the murder, the interest shifts to the question of whether the women will cover up for Minnie.

The distinction between what the men and the women look for is paralleled in the distinction between the morality of the men and the women. The men stand for law and order and for dominance (they condescend to the women, and the murdered Wright can almost be taken as a symbol of male dominance), whereas the women stand for mutual support or nurturing. Students might be invited to argue about why the women protect Minnie. Is it because women are nurturing? Or because they feel guilt for their earlier neglect of Minnie? Or because, being women, they know what her sufferings must have been like and feel that she acted justly? All of the above?

Mitsuye Yamada

To the Lady (p. 771)

First, some background: In 1942, the entire Japanese and Japanese American population on the Pacific coast—about 112,000 people—was relocated and incarcerated. More than two-thirds of the people moved were native-born citizens of the United States. (The 158,000 Japanese residents of the Territory of Hawaii were not affected.)

Immediately after the Japanese attack on Pearl Harbor, many journalists, the general public, Secretary of the Army Henry Stimson, and congressional delegations from California, Oregon, and Washington called for the internment. Although Attorney General Francis Biddle opposed it, on February 19, 1942, President Franklin D. Roosevelt signed Executive Order 9066, allowing military authorities "to prescribe military areas . . . from which any or all persons may be excluded." In practice, no persons of German or Italian heritage were disturbed, but the Japanese and Japanese Americans on the Pacific coast were rounded up (they were allowed to take with them "only that which can be carried") and relocated in camps. Congress, without a dissenting vote, passed legislation supporting the evacuation. A few Japanese Americans challenged the constitutionality of the proceeding but with no immediate success. (For two good short accounts, with suggestions for further readings, see the articles titled "Japanese Americans, wartime relocation of," in *Kodansha Encyclopedia of Japan,* 4:17–18, and "War Relocation Authority" in *Kodansha Encyclopedia of Japan,* 8:228. For a readable account of life in a camp, see Jeanne Wakatsuki Houston's *Farewell to Manzanar,* 1973.)

It may be interesting to read Mitsuye Yamada's poem aloud in class, *without* having assigned it for prior reading, and to ask students for their responses at various stages— after lines 4, 21, and 36. Lines 1 to 4 pose a question that perhaps many of us (young and old, and whether of Japanese descent or not) have asked, at least to ourselves. The question, implying a criticism of the victims, shows an insufficient awareness of Japanese or Japanese American culture of the period. It also shows an insufficient awareness of American racism; by implying that protest by the victims *could* have been effective, it reveals ignorance of the terrific hostility of whites toward persons of Japanese descent.

The first part of the response shows one aspect of the absurdity of the lady's question. Japanese and Japanese Americans were brought up not to stand out in any way (certainly not to make a fuss) and to place the harmony of the group (whether the family or society as a whole) above individual expression. Further, there was nothing that these people could effectively do, even if they had shouted as loudly as Kitty Genovese did. For the most part, they were poor, had no political clout, and were hated and despised as Asians. The absurdity of the view that they could have resisted effectively is comically stated in "should've pulled myself up from my / bra straps" (echoing the red-blooded American ideal of pulling oneself up by one's bootstraps), but of course, the comedy is bitter.

Then the speaker turns to "YOU," nominally the "lady" of the title but in effect also the reader, and by ironically saying what we would have done, points out what in fact we did not do. (The references to a march on Washington and letters to Congress are clear enough, but most students will not be aware of the tradition that the King of Denmark said that he would wear a Star of David [line 27] if Danish Jews were compelled by Nazis to wear the star.)

Thus far, the speaker has put the blame entirely on the white community, especially since lines 5 to 21 strongly suggest that the Japanese Americans *couldn't* do anything except submit. Yet the poem ends with a confession that because Japanese Americans docilely subscribed to "law and order"—especially the outrageous Executive Order 9066 —they were in fact partly responsible for the outrage committed against them. The last line of the poem, "All are punished," is exactly what Prince Escalus says at the end of *Romeo and Juliet.* Possibly the echo is accidental, though possibly the reader is meant to be reminded of a play, widely regarded as "a tragedy of fate," in which the innocent are victims of prejudice.

This poem can be the starting point for an argumentative research paper concerning the internment (or was it "relocation"?) of Japanese Americans during World War II. Was the internment justifiable, given the circumstances? Was it legal? Is the compensation voted by Congress in 1988 appropriate? (The law promised $20,000 to each of the 75,000 survivors of the camps.)

Peer wants to be himself, so he casts off relationship after relationship—friends, business associates, family members—in an effort to be himself. Late in the play Ibsen shows Peer with an onion; he peels off layer after layer, and, of course, he finds no internal hard core, no self within; the self consists of relationships with others.

You may know a good deal more about Buddhism than we do, but in case you have no familiarity with it, we offer some background.

Very briefly, Buddhism was founded in the sixth century B.C.E. by Siddhartha, crown prince of the Shakya kingdom in what is now the India-Nepal border. Rich, married, and a father, he became dissatisfied with his perception of illness, old age, and death, and he abandoned his princely life to learn if there was more to life than the usual course of birth, death, and (in the creed he grew up in) rebirth—an endless merry-go-round of suffering. After living for six years as an ascetic, he abandoned asceticism, took normal food, meditated, and became a Buddha (Enlightened One). Henceforth, he was known as Shakyamuni (the Sage of the Shakya) or the historical Buddha.

The enlightenment he achieved had to do with his perception of reality. We can hardly be expected to explain exactly what this is, but the gist is that unhappiness in life comes from craving—from a desire to satisfy the self, which is conceived of as something opposed to the rest of the universe.

Buddhism, of course, is immensely complicated. It has a long history, it has developed many schools, and there is much argument about terms such as *self,* but we can probably say that the heart of Buddhism is the belief that suffering is omnipresent. The Buddha taught that the way to escape suffering is by awareness of the Four Noble Truths:

1. All existence is characterized by suffering; the human condition (though it includes temporary pleasures) is one of physical and psychological disease.

2. Suffering is caused by attachment, by a thirst for selfish pleasure, and orientation to the transient.

3. Suffering can be eliminated, but only by ceasing to crave.

4. One can cease to crave only by leading a disciplined, moral life, and this is set forth in the Eightfold Path, which takes one from the realm of suffering to Nirvana.

With some hesitation—this is getting complicated—we give one version of the Eightfold Path, which the Buddha taught in his first sermon. These are not eight successive stages but are eight practices that are to be engaged in simultaneously. We are aware that each of the following points needs considerable amplification, and it may be that you will want some students to give reports on some aspects of Buddhism.

1. Right view (understanding reality, which means understanding the Four Noble Truths)

2. Right intention (resolution to renounce desire, and to commit to goodwill and harmlessness)

3. Right speech (avoidance of lying, angry words, and gossip)

4. Right action (avoidance of harming, dishonesty, and sexual misconduct)

5. Right livelihood (avoidance of harmful ways of making a living, including dealing with weapons, living creatures, and intoxicants)

6. Right effort (cultivation of what is wholesome)

7. Right mindfulness (clear consciousness, arrived at by contemplating the body, feeling, and states of mind)

8. Right concentration (a stage in meditation in which mental activity ceases and the mind is united with the object of meditation)

Bertrand Russell

The Happy Life (p. 789)

Some students may be distressed by Bertrand Russell's use of the pronoun *he* ("the moralist . . . he") where we would now say *he or she*. If the issue comes up in class, it is easy to inform students that the use of the masculine pronoun in a generic sense was common when Russell wrote this essay in 1930.

Russell's view of happiness seems to us to be pretty close to the mainline classical view, as found in Aristotle's *Nicomachean Ethics:* Happiness is not a matter of good sensations and certainly not a matter of pleasant sensations rooted in ignorance. (In *A Tale of a Tub*, Jonathan Swift famously defines happiness as "a perpetual possession of being well-deceived" and "felicity" as "the serene peaceful state of being a fool among knaves.") If Americans are asked to quote a line or phrase that has "happiness" in it, they probably will quote the Declaration of Independence, which speaks of "the pursuit of happiness," but Russell, like Aristotle, sees happiness as a by-product, something that comes out of an active relationship with others. For Aristotle, happiness is not something to be pursued, and it certainly is not gained by monitoring one's thoughts by "mindfulness training" (a term we saw on a poster advertising a course in how to be happy). Nor is it a matter of physical sensations (something experienced while drinking cold beer or taking a hot bath). Rather, happiness is a state of equanimity that incidentally arises from living the virtuous life, and the virtuous life is a life lived in society.

For Russell, happiness is not a matter of selfless behavior (the narrow moralistic view). Indeed, according to him, for the active person (we almost said "for the active man"), "the whole antithesis between self and the rest of the world . . . disappears as soon as we have any genuine interest in persons or things outside ourselves" (para. 2).

Russell probably would not have thought that he had much in common with the Dalai Lama, but we think some of our comments below on the essay by the Dalai Lama may also be relevant to Russell's essay.

The Dalai Lama and Howard C. Cutler

Inner Contentment (p. 791)

The Dalai Lama, in many of his writings, returns to a basic theme: Ignorance conditions us to think that we are separate entities, opposed to a hostile universe. The conquest of greed (or avarice), hatred (or aversion), and delusion (or ignorance)—what Buddhists call "the three poisons"—frees us from a condition of suffering or craving ("dis-ease," Sanskrit *dukkha*) and leads us to a twofold condition of *wisdom* (we see through the delusions of self-preoccupation, and we experience bliss) and *compassion* (we express our bliss in a concern for others). That is, in this enlightened condition, we are free from self-concern— from a desire to maintain our sense of ego and from our hatred of anything that opposes our concept of ourself—and in this new state, we express an unselfish concern for others and can achieve happiness.

We want to offer a few additional words about "the self," especially because so many students wish "to find themselves" or "to be true to themselves." (This issue is raised in Danielle Crittenden's essay on page 798.) We sometimes quote Robert Frost's "The Silken Tent," which begins, "She is as in a field a silken tent," and goes on to describe the tent, supported by a central cedar pole, that "is loosely bound / By countless silken ties of love and thought / To everything on earth the compass round." That is, the tent is supported— stands as a tent—because of its ties to the ground. It is what it is, it is a self, because of its connections with others. An episode in Henrik Ibsen's play *Peer Gynt* also comes to mind.

Mill was a qualitative hedonist; he believed that some pleasures were better than others, by which he did not mean merely that they were more pleasant. Jeremy Bentham was a quantitative hedonist; he believed that, ceteris paribus, the more pleasant some experience is, the better it is.

As to question 8, an argument to the effect that we are happier today than we were three centuries ago might proceed by asserting that a higher percentage of people (say, in the United States) are today able to fulfill their desires than was true in 1700, and successful pursuit of one's desires is (part of) what we mean by being happy. The issue, of course, is an empirical one and is not open to direct verification or falsification. Still, one might hope to find evidence in journals, diaries, and letters for the years 1650 through 1750 that reveal the miseries so many people suffered but no longer do. Take, as just one example, smallpox—a deadly disease at that time, and now virtually wiped out.

The answer to question 3 depends, of course, on how much prior knowledge or conjecture about happiness you have been exposed to. We confess to not (yet) having read McMahon's book, *Happiness: A History* (2006), and we doubt whether many who read this entry will have done so either. So each of us will have to answer this question as we see fit and will have to do so without being exposed to the most recent scholarship on the topic.

Question 5 asks us to think about whether suffering is our natural state. From an evolutionary point of view, it seems highly unlikely. Why would we want to prolong our lives to the point of ability to procreate if we were miserable all or most of the time? McMahon wants to go farther; he thinks we were "meant to be" happy. Are we wrong to think we sense intelligent design lurking in the background? In any case, that may not be McMahon's intention.

Epictetus

From *The Handbook (p. 786)*

Our headnote is longer than usual because we try to provide students with a brief introduction to stoicism. Students who have seen the film *Gladiator* (2000) with Richard Harris as Marcus Aurelius will doubtless be able to supplement our comments. We didn't want to overload the introductory note, so we didn't introduce the stoic idea of *apatheia.* But in classroom discussion of the stoic indifference to everything external (riches or poverty, sickness or health) because such things are neither good nor bad but merely indifferent, you may want to introduce this word. (The Greek word for "lack of feeling" gives us our word *apathy,* though the meanings are somewhat different, since the English word suggests a kind of slackness or inattentiveness rather than a principled dispassionateness.)

Some of the passages that we quote from *The Handbook* are old favorites of ours, from our student days—which is not to say that we claim to have ever lived the stoic life. Indeed, another favorite passage of ours is Jonathan Swift's bitter comment, "The Stoical scheme of supplying our Wants by lopping off our Desires is like cutting off our feet when we want shoes."

We confess that we are a trifle uneasy about including a stoic piece in a section on happiness, since the stoics were not concerned with happiness. They were concerned with duty and virtue: One does one's duty (that is, one acts rationally), and having done one's duty (having behaved virtuously), one then might experience pleasure, but pleasure is not the goal and indeed pleasure is not even a good. It is our impression that with the stoics, we are pretty close to Voltaire's view at the end of *Candide:* "We must cultivate our garden" ([I] faut cultiver notre jardin).

A topic for discussion: Has Thoreau said anything that may lead you to change the way you dress? If so, explain. If not, do you think he has nothing to say, or do you think he does indeed make some good points but you nevertheless will choose to ignore him?

[*We do not ride on the railroad; it rides upon us.*]

Admittedly, Thoreau sometimes can be a bit of a nag, but we think this passage is quite wonderful. Although in our seventh question we suggest that a student may doubt the wisdom of Thoreau's assertion that "Our life is frittered away by detail," we nevertheless do see his point, and we do experience the force of "let your affairs be as two or three, and not a hundred or a thousand . . . and keep your accounts on your thumb nail." And then he really gets going, with the claim (midway in the passage) that the nation "lives too fast." This gets him to the railway—the jetliner of his day—and to an especially wonderful passage about the nation living too fast:

> It lives too fast. Men think that it is essential that the *Nation* have commerce, and export ice, and talk through a telegraph, and ride thirty miles an hour, without a doubt, whether *they* do or not; but whether we should live like baboons or like men, is a little uncertain. If we do not get out sleepers, and forge rails, and devote days and nights to the work, but go to tinkering upon our *lives* to improve *them*, who will build railroads? And if railroads are not built, how shall we get to heaven in season? But if we stay at home and mind our business, who will want railroads? We do not ride on the railroad; it rides upon us. Did you ever think what those sleepers are that underlie the railroad? Each one is a man, an Irishman, or a Yankee man. The rails are laid on them, and they are covered with sand, and the cars run smoothly over them. They are sound sleepers, I assure you. And every few years a new lot is laid down and run over; so that, if some have the pleasure of riding on a rail, others have the misfortune to be ridden upon. And when they run over a man that is walking in his sleep, a supernumerary sleeper in the wrong position, and wake him up, they suddenly stop the cars, and make a hue and cry about it, as if this were an exception. I am glad to know that it takes a gang of men for every five miles to keep the sleepers down and level in their beds as it is, for this is a sign that they may sometime get up again.

Surely there is great power in Thoreau's almost comic reduction of the nation's "commerce" to exporting ice, talking through the telegraph, and riding an astounding thirty miles in an hour. This gets Thoreau to the irony—OK, to the sarcasm (but it's clever)—of "And if railroads are not built, how shall we get to heaven in season?" For us, the most memorable part of the passage is the part beginning "We do not ride on the railroad; it rides upon us." He continues, punning on "sleepers" (railway ties, and persons who are sleeping): The ties are laid down at the cost of human lives, chiefly lives exhausted in the effort, but occasionally a life is quite literally destroyed, accidentally, in the process of constructing the railroad. The passage is worth quoting again:

> Did you ever think what those sleepers are that underlie the railroad? Each one is a man, an Irishman, or a Yankee man. The rails are laid on them, and they are covered with sand, and the cars run smoothly over them. They are sound sleepers, I assure you.

We have sometimes read this passage aloud in class, and it seems to us—though perhaps we are pushing things—that Thoreau is conveying something of the sound of the railroad through repetition, especially through the abundant *m*'s, *n*'s, and *r*'s, indeed through the repetition of "sleepers" and "man." Try saying aloud "Each one is a man, an Irishman, or a Yankee man," and see if you don't agree that Thoreau is somehow evoking the sound of a railroad train.

Darrin M. McMahon

In Pursuit of Unhappiness (p. 783)

In regard to questions 2 and 6, a hedonist is anyone who believes that pleasure is the only or the highest good. The term *hedonism* comes from the Greek *hedone*, "happiness" or "pleasure." In Aristotle, *hedone* is contrasted with *eudaimonia*, "well-being." John Stuart

Henry David Thoreau

Selections from Walden *(p. 778)*

[As for Clothing]

Given the passages about clothing, this may be a convenient place for us to list all of the chief uses of clothing that we can think of. Probably the three chief functions can be listed as:

1. Protection or comfort;

2. Concealment, and

3. Display.

But we divide Display into

   a. Identification, and

   b. Ornament or individualization.

And we add yet another relatively unimportant category:

   4. Utility.

The categories are not exclusive and coordinated, but we think they are useful anyway.

- **Protection or comfort**: against heat and cold, rain, thorns, weapons, hockey pucks, and so on

- **Concealment**: for protection (e.g., camouflage uniforms), but it can also conceal to serve the needs of modesty.

- **Identification**: to identify the wearer's sex (or at least it used to do this) and status, for example, as a member of the idle rich, a proper business executive, a student, an admiral. The uniforms of athletes—say, football players—protect, and they also identify. Speaking of uniforms, it is worth noting that although a uniform can establish authority (a police officer, a priest, a nurse), a uniform often subordinates (e.g., prisoner, bellhop).

- **Ornament or individualization**: the cut of clothing—to say nothing of the fabric, jewelry, and accessories—can serve to ornament for aesthetic reasons (probably to establish status) or to individualize. If clothing can serve the purposes of modesty by concealing, it can also work the other way, by heightening sexual attractiveness. That is, clothing can reveal as well as conceal, or, to put it a little differently, clothes can emphasize by elaborately hiding. Without our clothing, we look pretty much alike; with clothing, we can make ourselves distinctive. Note that in tropical climates, where little clothing seems to be worn, body painting was common, presumably revealing a desire to enhance the all-too-ordinary body.

- **Utility**: providing pockets and belts, useful for carrying stuff

It happens, by chance, that the preceding comments were written only a day before a young man of our acquaintance, who had been accepted by the undergraduate college of business administration at a midwestern university, received information telling him that an orientation session would be held on such-and-such a day, and that he was expected to wear "business casual" clothing. "Business casual" for men, it seems, means a blazer, a button-down shirt, no tie, and khaki pants. The prospect of wearing these items gave this pre-freshman a good deal of pleasure, especially since he did not own a blazer and therefore he told his parents that he had to buy one, as well some additional shirts with button-down collars. (We refrained from quoting Thoreau: "Beware of all enterprises that require new clothes, and not rather a new wearer of clothes," para. 2.) But is it possible that Thoreau did not see that when one wears new clothes, one may become a new person?

28
What Is Happiness? (p. 774)

Thoughts about Happiness, Ancient and Modern (p. 774)

We have never taught any of these quotations, but it is our guess that students will enjoy writing about them, perhaps by amplifying one, by opposing one, or by juxtaposing two quotations.

Some of the passages are sternly moral (such as Shaw's "We have no more right to consume happiness without producing it than to consume wealth without producing it"); some seem almost proverbial (Mill's "Ask yourself whether you are happy, and you cease to be so"; Wharton's "If only we'd stop trying to be happy, we could have a pretty good time"; Frost's "Happiness makes up in height for what it lacks in length"); some are so worldly wise that they seem cynical (Graham Greene's "Point me out the happy man and I will point you out either egotism, selfishness, evil—or else an absolute ignorance"); some—but what is the use of classifying these engaging observations? We do think, to repeat, that students will enjoy taking one of them as a text and amplifying it or perhaps offering counterexamples.

Daniel Gilbert

Does Fatherhood Make You Happy? (p. 775)

Reminder: The essay was published a few days before Father's Day, hence the references to the holiday. Note, too, by the way, that Gilbert not only begins by referring to the holiday but also ends by returning to it, which is to say that he employs a writer's age-old strategy for wrapping things up: Return, via an allusion or a verbal echo, to something said in the opening paragraph. (We have met an occasional teacher of composition who dismisses such a strategy, saying, "I don't want my students to write according to a formula." But real writers in the real world *do* use these time-tested formulas—or rhetorical patterns or templates or strategies, or whatever one wants to call them.)

The essay is perhaps the most lighthearted piece in the book, and it must have been recognized as lighthearted by readers of the *New York Times*, but students—such is their earnestness and perhaps their fear when they confront a textbook—sometimes can hardly believe that the essay is meant to be entertaining as well as informative. One hopes, however, that students hear a genial note by the end of the first paragraph, when they read that after receiving gifts of after-shave and neckties, "millions of fathers . . . have precisely the same thought at precisely the same moment: 'My children,' they think in unison, 'make me happy.'"

Under the joking, however, there is a serious point. We are not sure that what Gilbert says about fatherhood is true, but we are fairly certain that he is right when he says that a baseball game that is tedious for eight-and-a-half innings because there was no scoring can become a wonderful game—in memory—when a batter hits a home run in the bottom of the ninth. As Gilbert puts it, "Memories are dominated by their most powerful—and not their most typical—instances" (para. 9). Gilbert is rather prosaically saying pretty much what Robert Frost said more epigrammatically, "Happiness makes up in height what it lacks in length."

Judy Brady

I Want a Wife (p. 801)

Incidental passages of satire, employing an ironic voice, appear throughout the book, but Judy Brady's essay, like Jonathan Swift's "A Modest Proposal" in Chapter 5, is satiric from beginning to end. Since our book is chiefly about argument (reasoning) rather than about the broader topic of persuasion, we discuss irony very briefly. And because of our emphasis on engaging the audience's goodwill by presenting oneself as benign, and because of Carl Rogers's point about reducing the sense of threat to the reader (see Chapter 12), we advise students to think twice before they use irony in their arguments. Still, Brady's essay offers an opportunity to talk about the power of verbal irony or satire—in Frank O'Connor's definition, "The intellectual dagger opposing the real dagger."

In talking about this satire, one can point out that in "I Want a Wife," as in much other satire, the persona more or less appears as an innocent eye, a speaker who merely describes, in a simple, objective way, what is going on. (The reader, not the speaker, says, "This is outrageous." The speaker never explicitly states her thesis.) Thus, in the essay Brady is not a creature with a name but merely a member of a class. She is simply "a Wife." We then get the terrifying list of things that a Wife finds thrust on her. These are scarcely described in detail, but the mere enumeration of the chores becomes, by the volume of its unadorned accumulation, comic — and stinging. One is reminded of John Dryden's comment, in *Origin and Progress of Satire* (1692), distinguishing between invective (direct abuse) and verbal irony:

> How easy is it to call "rogue" and "villain," and that wittily. But how hard to make a man appear a fool, a blockhead, or a knave, without using any of those opprobrious terms.

Whether things have changed since 1971, when Brady's essay first appeared in *Ms.* magazine, is a question that might be argued. One might also ask (though of course one doesn't expect a balanced view in satire) if things in 1971 really were the way Brady saw them. Did marriage really offer nothing to a wife? No love, no companionship, no security? Were all husbands childish and selfish, and all wives selfless?

Is he correct in mocking the right to happiness by comparing it with the right to good luck or the right to be six feet tall? (See questions 4 and 5.) It can't just be that our luck and our height are not within our control; many things in life are not within our control, but they involve no rights; for example, we have no control over our age, but that is not because we have no right to being the age we happen to be. Perhaps it is because the things to which we have a right are terribly important to our status as rational, autonomous agents, whereas our age or height or luck does not play such a central role. (We might imagine a world in which everyone did have a right to be six feet tall, but that is another story altogether—though it would be a useful exercise to think of the circumstances in which such a right would exist.)

Question 6 takes us into a discussion of legal and moral rights: A legal right is a right created by some form of legal enactment—by statutory, judicial, or constitutional law that gives one a legal claim, such as to a piece of real estate. A moral right is any right created or recognized by moral theory or principle—for example, a moral claim based on a promise, which may or may not also be enforceable by law. One might have a moral and a legal claim to the same thing, just as one might lack both a moral and a legal claim to something.

We do not agree with Lewis (see question 7) that an alleged right to happiness is really an alleged right to sexual happiness. He offers no convincing evidence on the point, and we can think of none. Were he correct, no one would have a right to happiness before about the age of twelve. That seems to us quite unconvincing.

We are not biologists and so our answer to question 8 is little better than an educated guess. We can see how monogamy for women might well be a biological necessity; there seems to us good reason to believe that women in general are hardwired toward monogamy, whereas men in general are hardwired to spread their sperm as broadly as possible. Lewis is like us, not a biologist, and so his pronouncements about women's sexual nature need to be greeted cautiously. We grant that he gives a clear and persuasive argument in paragraph 28 in support of his claim about monogamy.

Danielle Crittenden

About Love (p. 798)

We include this piece for several reasons: We think it is readable; we think it is provocative; we think the point about "being oneself" is immensely important; and we think it will perhaps especially interest older students, especially those who are or who have been married.

In our discussion (in this manual) of the selection by the Dalai Lama, we talk at some length about this business of the "self"—we raise the idea that perhaps there is no "self" apart from the relationships we build with others—so we will not go into the matter here, but we urge you to consider assigning the Dalai Lama's essay along with Danielle Crittenden's. We also urge you to look back at the first selection in this chapter, "Thoughts about Happiness," where you will find several quotations that fit nicely with Crittenden's argument. For instance, the comment by Mary Wollstonecraft Shelley and the second comment by Shaw ("We have no more right to consume happiness without producing it than to consume wealth without producing it") imply that happiness is a product of a virtuous interaction—not of the preservation of one's independence.

We have not taught this essay, but it is our guess that it will provoke lively discussion and interesting written responses.

By these practices, it is said, one extinguishes the passions (which produce ignorant actions) and arrives at enlightenment.

Attempts to eliminate passion—to detach oneself from the things of this world—are not, of course, limited to Buddhism. One can easily find Christian texts that urge renunciation:

> But I say unto you, That whosoever looketh on a woman to lust after her hath committed adultery with her already in his heart. / And if thy right eye offend thee, pluck it out, and cast it from thee: for it is profitable for thee that one of thy members should perish, and not that the whole body should be cast into hell. (Matthew 5:28–29)

> He that loveth father or mother more than me is not worthy of me: and he that loveth son or daughter more than me is not worthy of me. (Matthew 10:37)

> And everyone that hath forsaken houses, or brethren, or sisters, or father, or mother, or wife, or children, or lands, for my name's sake, shall receive an hundredfold, and shall inherit everlasting life. (Matthew 19:29)

We are not saying that in the matter of renunciation, Christianity and Buddhism are the same. We daily try (especially when we ask students to write a comparison) to keep in mind a remark by Bishop Joseph Butler: "Everything is what it is, and not another thing." Still, if some students find the Buddhist ideal of renunciation odd, we think it is worth citing some Christian texts that strike many people as no less odd.

C. S. Lewis

We Have No "Right to Happiness" (p. 794)

So C. S. Lewis tells us that we have no "right to happiness." Before complaining too loudly, consider the possible objections he might be raising. Perhaps we have no right to happiness because we have no rights at all. That's what Jeremy Bentham and John Stuart Mill would have said in the 1830s, had they been asked. Perhaps instead Lewis holds that we do have rights, but in the case of happiness we confuse a right to happiness with it being right to seek and preserve such happiness as we can obtain—and it is right to seek and preserve our happiness. There may be other possibilities, too.

The right to happiness has never been very popular with the theorists and manifestos purporting to state what our rights are. It doesn't appear in the French Declaration of the Rights of Man and Citizen (1789), and it is missing from the list of "natural rights" identified and defended by John Locke ("life, liberty, and property" [1690]). Nor was it mentioned in the Universal Declaration of Human Rights (1948). It appears only and famously in the American Declaration of Independence in the memorable phrase "the right to life, liberty and the pursuit of happiness."

These, however, are what we might call some of the political dimensions to an alleged right. Lewis's essay is not concerned with these dimensions at all (though he does discuss them briefly, in paragraphs 12–13). He is concerned with happiness in our private lives and the alleged right to happiness in that setting. He mocks the idea when he draws the parallel between this alleged right and "a right to good luck" (para. 6) or "a right to be six feet tall" (para. 6). Lewis rehearses some general ideas about our rights in paragraph 7, correctly pointing out that some rights are lawfully protected freedoms and other rights are lawful claims to certain benefits or services. The American legal philosopher W. N. Hohfeld added two further kinds of rights: powers, as with Congress's power to raise taxes, and immunities, as with the immunity against self-incrimination specified in the Fifth Amendment to the federal Constitution. This fourfold set of rights has become the standard conception of rights both moral and legal. It seems to play no role in Lewis's understanding of the alleged right to happiness.